Complete Book of
TAROT
SPREADS

Evelin Burger
& Johannes Fiebig

Sterling Publishing Co., Inc.
NEW YORK

Library of Congress Cataloging-in-Publication Data

Burger, Evelin.
    [Tarot Praxis. English]
    Complete book of Tarot spreads / by Evelin Burger &
Johannes Fiebig.
        p.   cm.
    ISBN 0-8069-9505-X
    1. Tarot.   2. Fortune-telling by cards.   I. Title.
BF1879.T2B84513   1997
133.3´2424—dc21   96–52303
                                                   CIP

                7   9   10   8

    Published by Sterling Publishing Company, Inc.
    387 Park Avenue South, New York, N.Y. 10016
    Originally published in Germany by Königsfurt Verlag
            under the title *Tarot Praxis*
            © 1995 Königsfurt Verlag
English version and translation © 1997 by Sterling Publishing Company, Inc.
        Distributed in Canada by Sterling Publishing
    ℅ Canadian Manda Group, One Atlantic Avenue, Suite 105
            Toronto, Ontario, Canada M6K 3E7
    Distributed in Great Britain and Europe by Cassell PLC
    Wellington House, 125 Strand, London WC2R 0BB, England
    Distributed in Australia by Capricorn Link (Australia) Pty Ltd.
P.O. Box 6651, Baulkham Hills, Business Centre, NSW 2153, Australia
        Manufactured in the United States of America
                All rights reserved

        Sterling ISBN 0-8069-9505-X

Table of Contents

Preface

Tarot combines beautifully a sense of fun with a sense of seriousness to complement freedom and personal commitment. It will also improve your intuition when you use specific methods and compare your personal experiences with otherwise seemingly rigid traditions of Tarot interpretation.

This book will help you maximize your intuition by teaching you a methodical use of Tarot cards. It will increase your familiarity with the cards and help you see the potential and inner connections inherent in them. Since Tarot cards can be considered a "mirror," it's our hope that the end effect will be a greater self-awareness and self-intimacy. It may also make it easier for you to find the answers to your personal desires and fears.

Being lucky has nothing to do with chance. It depends more on the courage to confront the often hidden realities of your life head-on. It also takes a certain know-how to see nuances more clearly as well as to find bridges and new direction. This book contains the tools for using Tarot to help you see and find them.

Many of the new approaches here were gathered from Johannes' seminars over the years. Some we have fully developed from other sources. They are presented with over one hundred layouts that we have collected to accompany and support you on your journey.

Have fun with Tarot!

Evelin Burger & Johannes Fiebig

Chapter 1: Practicing Tarot

1. Guide and Introduction

Tarot cards are very old playing cards. In its contemporary form, the Tarot deck contains seventy-eight cards. This book offers you a guide for reading these Tarot cards. It will show you what you may experience with them and how to become familiar with their inner connections.

Whether you read this book from cover to cover, use parts of it, or use it as a reference book, it will mysteriously yet clearly strengthen your personal magical powers with the cards when you practice with them.

For Beginners

If you need an introduction to the basics of Tarot, including the conventional forms of interpretation, start from this chapter. If you are a beginner but want to start playing immediately, read pages 20 to 26. Begin with a layout starting on page 47.

For the Advanced

For the more experienced, we recommend that you start on page 27. This chapter on theme cards discusses "Stress," "Luck," "Entrance," "Unknown," etc. The different layouts begin on page 47.

For the Expert

We recommend that experts read the section beginning on page 30, which discusses techniques for interpreting Tarot, and Chapter 3 (Tarot and Astrology), which offers exercise tips. Layouts that are known only to smaller circles (starting on page 47) will be of particular interest as well.

Many people refer to their card of the day, or day card, on a regular basis. What is it that makes Tarot so intriguing? Why is it so important for and attractive to so many people?

Working with Chance

Working with Tarot is a process that combines "working with chance," the search for meaning in ancient symbols and archetypes, and a person's own sense of wonder.

A Tarot layout is like a dream or a movie which we are a part of. It is like a puzzle or a work of art, and we are a piece of that puzzle. It is like an encounter with our own magical powers.

From a practical point of view, reading Tarot cards for yourself means coming face-to-face with yourself. It is this moment of "meeting" that makes the day card such a favorite for many people. Self-awareness, defining your position, and finding new directions are exercised every day so that it is like making an appointment with yourself. Exercises for working daily spreads start on page 47.

Reading Tarot cards is also like a declaration of love—a declaration that we love ourselves. And as "The Lovers" card indicates, Tarot gives us a chance to come to terms with ourselves by seeing ourselves from a higher level.

In most cases, just paying attention to our own feelings is healing. Desires and fears, troubles and joy are being expressed. Through Tarot cards, experiences that may be difficult to put into words are seen more clearly and in greater detail. Whatever is moving our hearts will find its expression here. And whatever we are thinking about will seem to appear as if it is displayed on the television screen.

Tarot Cards: Expression and TV Screen

Of course, the magic of Tarot unfolds best when you continuously work with it. For instance, dream interpretations are more interesting when you take a look at a series of dreams rather than one single dream. The same holds true for Tarot. Having a daily spread is one way of establishing continuity.

Advantages of the Day Card

Working with a day card is highly recommended, especially for the beginner. It offers the best and most practical entry into Tarot. For the more advanced, it unfolds its full meaning and makes it possible for you to detect your personal pattern and associations. Experienced people use the day card to find, among other things, specific blind spots and personal resistance, as well as new chances and unexpected "directions" (personal clarification and tasks), in their life.

Dated Instructions

Instructions about how to handle Tarot cards—do you pull a card from the left? how must you shuffle the cards? the do's and don'ts about what kind of questions to ask, instructions on how long a given interpretation is valid, and so on—are all outdated. Even such calculations as figuring and interpreting a personality card are losing their appeal.

Those kinds of instructions are also included in this book only for the sake of completeness. But how can pulling and calculating a personality card compare to the process of discovering and watching your personality unfold, or dealing with personal desires and fears?

Tarot is a language of symbols. The magic of the symbols is a mirror, for the magic is in all of us. It becomes apparent as soon as we experience and learn about our place between heaven and earth.

The Magic of Symbols/The Magic of the Person

What you won't find in this book are layouts designed to discover how many "good" and "bad" cards they contain. You will also search in vain for "advice" about how to judge a layout by the number of "higher" cards (Major Arcana and cards from the Minor Arcana with higher numbers). People who want to make decisions or draw conclusions based on these might just as well roll dice.

What Is Not in This Book: A Pair of Dice

Tarot is about encountering certain experiences, contents, and meanings. If you are prepared for such an encounter, Tarot cards will open your eyes. They will increase the possibility for you to grasp more diverse and infinite realities. In addition to being a mirror of yourself, Tarot cards are also a mirror of all the other levels and facets of reality. Approaching and using Tarot cards with this understanding will then become a training ground and, eventually, a test for you to come to terms with these facets.

A Mirror of a Larger Reality

2. Basics

At the Beginning

Leaf through a Tarot deck. Look at the pictures. Pull out the card or cards that seem to especially "speak" to you.

Card of the Day

To pull your first card for the day, shuffle the cards in any way you like. Place the cards face down so that you won't be able to see the pictures and then, with attention and concentration, pull one card. This card is not dependent on or connected to any specific question. It represents the theme of the day or a magnifying glass for that day.

How the Tarot Cards Are Organized

When you look through the deck of cards, you will see that there are five categories. One group has titles ("The Magician," "The Lovers," "The Wheel of Fortune," etc.) while the other four groups are organized by a specific symbol (element). The symbols are called Wands, Cups, Swords, and Pentacles (in the Crowley cards the Pentacles are called "Disks"). Each symbol represents a "suit."

The Major Arcana

There are twenty-two cards of the Major Arcana (Arcana: secret; the "Big Secrets" or "The Big Stations of Tarot"). The four suits of symbols make up fifty-six cards that are part of the Minor Arcana.

You will recognize the twenty-two cards of the Major Arcana as follows: the cards in the Waite Tarot deck have roman numerals at the top of the picture and a title on the bottom. The cards in the Crowley Tarot deck have roman numerals at the top and the title at the bottom over a large, faint print of the word "Trumps." Most other versions of Tarot cards have similar variations.

The Cards of Your Astrological Sign

Check the table on pages 166–167 to find which Tarot cards belong to your astrological sign. Take a look at these cards and study them, or you can concentrated on just one card.

You might want to take this opportunity to find out what particular desire is closest to your heart. This will establish the "red thread" that will serve as a guide as you read and interpret Tarot cards for yourself.

The Guiding Thread Weaving Through a Tarot Layout

The Magic of the Moment

Since Tarot cards are like a mirror, you are a part of the picture in the card. Therefore, what you see in each individual picture is important. While you should make use of the interpretations provided in books, remember that your perception and your decision are what count.

- All seventy-eight cards have the same rank and are of equal importance. There is no such thing as an inherently good or bad card.

A "Good" or "Bad" Card?

- Every figure in each card—regardless of its subject or color, whether it is a man or woman, child or adult, human or animal—may represent you or a certain part of you.

- Pay attention to the perspective from which you observe a certain picture of a card. Are you identifying with the picture? If the picture has more than one figure, do you find yourself in all of them or some of them? Every card may also represent people, things, or events in your life. Determine your relationship to the individual figures or symbols in the picture.

How Do You See a Picture?

- Every card has "positive" and "negative" meanings. What you experience and feel at the moment you see the card is the determining factor. The interplay between the picture and reader puts the personal and relevant meaning of a card into concrete terms.

- It is very important that you focus your full attention on each individual card as it is turned over while simulta-

What Is Your Reaction?

neously observing your reaction and feelings. This will give you a direct, dynamic, and effective insight into the cards as well as your own self-awareness.

- Each card can have a different meaning with each encounter. Be open to its message.

- Physically hold the cards in your hand. Relax and breathe deeply. Concentrate on the question you have posed.

A Short ABC of Tarot

The seventy-eight cards of a Tarot deck are divided as follows: twenty-two stations (or cards) represent the Major Arcana and the fourteen stations (fifty-six cards) for each of the four suits (including the Court Cards) represent the Minor Arcana.

Arcana: Plural of Arkanum.

Arkanum: Latin for secret.

Divinatory: Discovering hidden knowledge, fortune-telling (literally: "proclaiming something godly," "sacred").

Cartomancy: Fortune-telling with the use of cards.

Court Cards: Queen, King, Knight, or Page (also called Princess). In Crowley Tarot deck: Queen, Prince, Knight, Princess.

Esoteric: The many different definitions of esoteric include: hidden, secret, not easily accessible (literally: "from within").

Mystic: The "direct connection to ultimate wisdom"; immediate and absolute experience of God and the world.

Mythology: The teaching of myth; also, specifically, ancient teaching of the gods.

Mythos: Fable, legend, archetype, (collective) ancient or early history.

Numbered Cards: The cards of the Minor Arcana that are numbered from 1 (= Ace) to 10.

Pagat: Early term for the card "I-The Magician."

Pentacles: Indicating talisman/mascot. Another name used for "Disks" in Tarot.

Pentagram: Five-pointed star on the "Pentacles" cards. It has many meanings: it is the "Quintessence" of the four elements and also is a cipher (a short-term sign for humans) where the five points of the star represent the head, hands, and feet.

Qabalah: "The Tradition"; ancient Jewish mysticism where the symbol of the "Tree of Life" as well as the mystical meaning of numbers and letters have great meaning. It exists in several variations and in several different traditions and branches.

Tarock, Tarok: Terms also used for Tarot.

Standard Interpretation

The first and most important thing to remember is that every card stands for itself. The configurations and symbols of a card's picture are much more important than its number and title.

No Pigeonholes

The twenty-two cards of the Major Arcana provide actual messages and, at the same time, present individual and collective models (archetypes). They are organized in several different systems (see also page 40).

Archetype

The Four Elements   Four elements are used for interpreting the fifty-six cards of the Minor Arcana. They are commonly assigned to four suits called: Wands, Cups, Swords, and Pentacles.

Fire   Wands represent the element of fire. They stand for willpower, vitality, zest for life, creativity, and growth. The world of the Wands is the world of initiation and action, engagement, accomplishments, and power. The Wands also deal with enterprise and entrance, identity, self-confidence, intuition, enthusiasm, and success. Aries, Leo, and Sagittarius are the astrological signs assigned to the Wands and the element of fire.

Water   Cups represent the element of water. They stand for the soul, inner life, and the unconscious. Their world is the world of feelings, moods, premonition, inner voices, and spiritual experiences. The Cups deal with intuitive awareness and knowledge, sense and meaning, joy, sadness, emptiness, and abundance. Cancer, Scorpio, and Pisces are the astrological signs assigned to the Cups and water.

Air   Swords represent the element of air. They stand for the mind, mental energy, awareness, knowledge, and intellect. The world of the Swords is the world of recognition, decision, ideas, and judgments. Swords deal with thought and imagination, the conscious and explicit awareness of the world and the self, originality, freedom, the learning processes, and clarity. Libra, Aquarius, and Gemini are the astrological signs assigned to the Swords and the element of air.

Earth   Pentacles (Disks/Coins) represent the element of earth. They stand for the body, physical experiences, practical and applied skills, and the creation of the concrete as well as your own environment. The world of the Pentacles is the world of results, facts and production, physical awareness, and impressions. Pentacles deal with work, nature and community, connections to the earth, self-awareness, and security. Capricorn, Taurus, and Virgo are the astrological signs assigned to the Pentacles and the element of earth.

Overview of Minor Arcana

Learning the meaning of the four elements is a good start towards interpreting the fifty-six cards of the Minor Arcana since most Tarot book authors agree on their assignment and description. We would like to give you our suggestions about the meaning of the Court and Numbered Cards.

Combining the description of the individual stations of the Minor Arcana with the interpretations of the four elements will give you a framework to aid, stimulate, and expand your personal interpretations.

Certain cards, such as those in the Crowley Tarot deck, have subtitles like "Success," Wealth," Disappointment," "Oppression," etc. These printed interpretations should not be used as the only description of a particular card.

Meaning of the Court Cards

All Court Cards represent the total potential of their respective element. They represent developed personalities and distinguish themselves by their characteristics.

Queen: Innovative, spontaneous, initiatory.
King/Prince: Thorough, solid, supportive.
Knight: Considering consequences, drawing conclusions, making changes.
Page/Princess: Playful, probing.

Pages 161ff discuss how the Court Cards in the Crowley Tarot deck compare to the Court Cards of other Tarot variations.

The Stations of the Numbered Cards

The following is an overview of the individual stations within the numbered cards. The numbers themselves have no specific significance.

1. (Ace) Origin and root. Both the goal and the

achievement. The characteristic power of the respective element. A curse and a blessing.

2. Strengthen or break open the power of the element. Differentiation, rupture, disentangling, contrast, and complementary.

3. The "crux of the matter": fundamental problem or sum (synthesis) of the respective element.

4. Stabilizing, organizing, and completion. New challenges and validation.

5. The personal quintessence of the respective element. Versatility and concentration.

6. Decision, consolidation, changes. The whole as an expression of complex contradictions. Joy or danger.

7. Test, sort out, refine. Take a look at what remains in the sieve and what does not. Critical phase, baffling, ambiguous, transformation, completion in relation to the respective element.

8. Conflict or harmony of weaknesses and strengths. Alternating blockage, balance, or support by different characteristics of the respective elements.

9. Maturing, scrutinizing, becoming aware. Self-awareness, searching, and finding personal autonomy in dealing with the respective element.

10. Fulfillment, goal, starting point. Many "tasks": the respective element provides the power to let go of and gain much.

Colors and Their General Meaning

The following symbolisms of the colors are also helpful for interpreting your own cards.

White: Beginning (in the sense of a blank page) or ending and healing. White shadow (animus). Union through the mind or new intellectual frontier.

Gray: Unawareness or deliberate indifference.

Black: The unknown, the center of the earth or of a situation; "black box," black shadow (anima), the dark side of the soul, or new psychological territory.

Red: Heart, soul, willpower, vitality.

Yellow: Sun, consciousness, zest for life; envy, mental dissonance.

Blue: Open sky/space and clear water; spirituality.

Green: Fresh, young, promising, inexperienced, immature.

Brown: Connected to nature and the earth, rooted in the soil, vegetative.

Violet: Experiencing boundaries; a mixture of blue and red.

3. Personality and Year Cards

Personality Card

Your personality card is calculated by adding the numbers of your birthday and then finding the Major Arcana card that corresponds to the sum. For instance, if your birthday is July 7, 1966, add $7+7+1+9+6+6 = 36$.

If the sum is from 1 to 21, the card from the Major Arcana with the corresponding number is your personality card. For example, if the sum is 19, your personality card is "XIX-The Sun." If the sum is 22, "XX-The Fool" is your personality card.

If the sum is greater than 22, then calculate the sum of the two digits. For instance, if your answer is 36, add $3+6 = 9$. Your personality card is then "IX-The Hermit."

Additional methods for finding your personality card are listed on page 75.

Character Card

To find your character card, calculate the sum of the digit(s) of your personality card. If the number of your personality card is from 1 to 9, the character card is identical to your personality card because you have only one digit. However, if the number of your personality card is from 10 to 22, you can then add the two digits to find your character card.

Variations

There are several variations on calculating a personality card. One variation, which has been suggested by some authors, tells you to first calculate an interim sum. Using the date July 7, 1966, $7+7+1966 = 1980$, which in turn will give you: $1+9+8+0 = 18$. "XVIII-The Moon" would then be your personality card. The first method, however, calculates "IX-The Hermit" as your personality card.

Which of these two methods is the correct one? If you calculate your personality card by adding each individual number, you would end up with the same number. Using our example—where our personality card is 18—if you add the two digits you will also get 9.

Other different methods have been presented in different Tarot books. It is best to take these variations into account instead of relying on only one method. We suggest using the direct method of calculation by adding each individual number, because this is the most common form.

Another hot debate is whether to include the first two digits of the year in your calculation. Some Tarot readers prefer to use only the last two digits—omitting the 19—which results in a different number. In our exercises, we will include the 19 in our calculations.

With or Without "19..."?

A year or growth card is calculated by using the numbers of the respective year instead of the numbers of your birthday. For instance, the sum of July 7, 1999, is $7+7+1+9+9+9 = 42$; $4+2 = 6$. "VI-The Lovers" is the respective year card for all people who celebrate their birthday on July 7, 1999.

Year or Growth Card

There is also a year card that belongs to everybody. We very simply add the numbers of the year. 1999 would be $1+9+9+9 = 28$; $2 + 8 = 10$. "X-The Wheel of Fortune" is therefore the year card for 1999.

Layouts for year cards can be found on pages 129ff.

A Year Card for Everybody

Remember that playing with numbers is and always should be stimulating and inspirational. After all, you can just as well find your personality and year cards by simply pulling or choosing them.

Playful Freedom

4. Large Layouts

Use all seventy-eight cards of the Tarot deck. The old method of only using twenty-two cards, which is still practiced sometimes, dates back to before 1910 when we only had the Major Arcana cards. Today, this general restriction is obsolete.

- Think about the question you want to pose to the Tarot cards. There are no restrictions on the kind of question you can ask.

- Remember that the cards act like a mirror. You can pose questions about a second or third person. The answers that the cards provide always take into consideration your understanding and relationship to that person. Whenever you are posing questions about other people, remember that you are always a part of the "game."

- Shuffle the cards as you like. All obligatory instructions, such as pulling cards from the left, mixing the cards by spreading them out on the table, fanning them out in a half circle or full circle, and so on, are unnecessary. Nothing gainsays personal rituals. But as Tarot book author Rachel Pollack once succinctly stated, "We should not forget that the actual magic is in the pictures themselves and not in the explanations." And neither, we would like to add, is it in how you construct a reading session. Some people use a candle and incense in order to get into the proper mood. Others do just as well by simply pulling a card for the day in the morning during breakfast, on the bus or train, or in the car on the way to work.

Interpreting Cards for Yourself

- When you read Tarot cards for yourself, it is customary and typical that you do your own mixing, laying out, describing, and interpreting of the cards. Whoever is posing the question should handle and interpret the cards as well as have the last word in the interpretation. Other people may be present for conversation, company, support, and, if need be, critiquing.

• Choose the layout you want beforehand. You may use those shown in Tarot books or you may design your own. Always choose the layout before you pose your question.

• Pull out the cards in any way you like. Place them face down in front of you in the design you have chosen.

• The cards are usually turned over one at a time. Only after you have viewed and interpreted each card should you proceed to the next.

• Everything that happens while questioning the cards can become part of the answer.

• All cards together in a layout give the answer to your question.

What Kind of Questions

Any questions that are important to you, like those you would write about in your journal, can be clarified with the help of Tarot cards. Stay with what is closest to your heart and what you are concerned about.

What Is Closest to Your Heart

The rule that you should not interpret Tarot cards for yourself or other close relatives dates back to the tradition of fortune-telling. This rule is invalid, in any case, when you use Tarot cards for yourself.

We can only read Tarot cards with, and not for, others—regardless if they are close relatives or friends. It would otherwise be like asking us to dream for or look into a mirror for them. We can only show and explain to them how they can do it for themselves.

Yes/No Question

Some authors have stated that you should not ask yes/no questions. But why not? It is perfectly fine to do so if a yes/no question is particularly important to you. Tarot cards are precisely good for what concerns you the most, what is mostly occupying your mind and thoughts. The answers, needless to say, must still be open.

Depending on the cards, you might find that you are guided in a certain direction or you might learn of the connections that are going hand in hand with your question.

Be Open to All Answers

Since the cards act as a mirror, the person who is posing the question should pull and interpret them.

If you are reading cards together with other people, the person who is posing the question may share the question with those present or keep it to him/herself. Either way has its advantages.

If the question is known, everyone can refer and deliberate over the pictures in the cards with the question in mind. If the question is not shared, then the people present—especially if they know each other well—may find new answers beyond the boundaries of the question in what the pictures and symbols are presenting.

Sum of the Digits or Quintessential Card

The answers to your questions are always found in the total layout, not in any one individual card. At the conclusion, you can calculate the sum of the digits of the cards in the layout. The Queen, King, Knight, Page, and The Fool count as 0; the Ace counts as 1.

The resulting number is treated in the same way as the personality card described on page 20. The Major Arcana card that corresponds to the calculated sum is the Quintessential card, or Quintessence.

The Meaning of the Quintessential Card

The Quintessential card adds nothing new to the completed layout. It can be viewed instead as a summary of it, as if giving the layout a title. Sometimes it may also act as a control card, testing the conclusion you have reached.

Important Questions Concerning Readings

Reverse Direction of the Layout

It is unnecessary to try to draw comparisons between a card placed on the table right side up or upside down. In contrast to fortune-telling and the older esoteric forms, today we assume that every card has a positive and negative meaning. Furthermore, before you can interpret a card you must keep in mind that every picture and every symbol represents a whole spectrum of potentially different ways of being perceived and understood.

Except for some special situations, we recommend that the cards be placed in front of the reader so that they can be seen right side up, regardless of the position they are in when the face-down cards are turned over.

The answer to your the question is always contained in the total layout, not in any individual card, even if a particular card might suggest the result of your efforts or summary.

How do we train ourselves to read this summary or overview of a total layout of, for instance, seven, ten, or thirteen cards? For many Tarot readers, this is not a problem. You can always relate to at least one story about a layout when dealing with one or several cards together.

"How Do I Find the Connection?"

For some Tarot readers, it makes a great difference if they are dealing with one card or a large, more complex layout. If you find yourself in this category, remember that everything that is happening while you are reading the Tarot cards represents a mirror. This mirror only brings out the conditions that also exist in everyday life. Search and find the connections that exist in your life.

Each reading that you do increases your awareness to make those connections.

Calculating the Quintessential card at the conclusion of your reading is particularly helpful (see page 24).

Temporal Relevance

How long a layout remains relevant is a difficult question to answer. Some issues are immediately being taken care of by the way a question is formulated and answered. Other questions may occupy your thoughts for months or years. And other life issues—like finding your purpose in life or dreams you have for your life—will accompany you throughout life, even if they take different forms and undergo many changes.

Therefore, books that say questions you pose are only valid for 4 to 6 weeks or for "the very near future" are as unfounded as all other opinions dating back to the fortune-telling tradition.

5. Theme Cards

Choosing a theme card helps you bring your own preferences and dislikes, suspicions and expectations into the process. To begin, spread the cards face up on the table in front of you. Look at all seventy-eight cards and, with your "heart and mind," pick the one card that seems to be most relevant to a certain theme or issue. During this process, the cards that jump out at you may be totally different from what you had expected.

Your Favorite Card

Which card, at this moment, is your favorite card? What do you notice about this card? What do you like about it? And what is it telling you?

It is a lot of fun to find your "favorite card," but this exercise has a deeper meaning. Take note of the kind of desires and interests that are at the center of your heart and mind at this time. Identifying and observing personal desires and fears while reading Tarot is like finding a guiding theme.

Stress Card

The stress card is also chosen, not pulled. Which card do you enjoy the least? Which card, at this point, is causing you the most stress? What are you noticing about this card? What is it that makes you feel ill at ease when this card has both positive or negative connotations?

At first, you may not be comfortable or think it useful to look for a stress card in the same way you are asking for your favorite card. But your desires and fears are being addressed and expressed in the language of Tarot symbols. Nothing better could happen to you! Furthermore, each stress card has a corresponding lucky card.

First, take a good look at your stress card. Determine what is in this card that stands for the stress of the day. Is there by any chance a positive side to this stress card?

Could there be needs that are hidden behind the stress? In the larger context, a stress card may be important for your growth.

The lucky card is one step beyond the stress card (stress card + 1). For example, if your stress card is Wands V, then your lucky card is Wands VI. If stress card = XV-The Devil, then lucky card = XVI-The Tower. If stress card = Swords X, then lucky card = Ace of Swords. After X, a new circle begins with the Ace. The sequence of the Court Cards is as follows: Queen, King, Knight, and Page.

Additional information about lucky cards is on page 172 ("Tarot and Astrology").

Learning Assignment

In the process of making decisions and gaining insight it is very effective to find a "learning assignment" card for a given situation. You choose this card the same way you choose the theme card.

The Unknown

In times of change, it is also useful to choose a card for what will be new or is still unknown.

Setting a Card Aside

Look for a card and set it aside for a specific date in the future. This card has no influence on the present time, but it may help you make the transition to some situation at a later date more easily.

Blind Spots

The "unknown" card also represents insight into our blind spots. More on this on subject is discussed on page 94.

Entrance Cards

In one of her books, Rachel Pollack lists seven or eight cards as entrance cards that, in her experience, are the doors to a deeper self-awareness. It is, however, important that you take into consideration two different points of view.

The first one is that every one of the seventy-eight cards is suitable as a door or key to deeper understanding and higher awareness. In this sense, you should not limit yourself to only a few cards. On the other hand, and according to our experiences, it is true that only a few cards have this certain significance for each Tarot reader. The number could be five, six, or even ten cards.

Every one of us has his/her very own "entrance cards." How can we recognize them?

These personal "entrance cards" can neither be chosen nor pulled. The only way to find them is to ask, to the best of your ability and knowledge, which of the seventy-eight cards you recognize as absolutely and only positive, or absolutely and only negative. Those cards that you find very hard to recognize, not just for their one meaning but their double meaning, are pointing to a blind spot as well as a personal "entrance."

How You Can Recognize Your Entrance Cards

6. Reading for Yourself

Interpretation and Its Two Components

Interpreting Tarot language is fundamentally based on two components. Both are equally important and must come together for a proper interpretation of a card (this meeting or integrating is one of the meanings of the Greek word *symbolon*). One component can not be substituted for the other. What are they?

Tradition and Our Own Understanding

One is called the personal component. The second part refers to the previous tradition of symbols and their variations.

As far as tradition is concerned, we mostly rely on books and previous studies. For the personal component, we have to rely on our own thought processes and our personal experiences with Tarot symbols. Only we can determine where we have to begin and where the focus of our current concerns is.

Some Tarot readers study Tarot books before they begin to develop their own interpretation. Others do just the reverse. They rely on their own (daily) involvement with Tarot until they have reached some clarity and certainty about their personal method of interpretations before they refer to books for additional input.

Whichever approach you use, it is imperative that you use both components.

Practicing Association

Associations Are Uncensored Ideas

Look at the picture or symbol on a card with undivided attention and without forming an immediate opinion. Collect whatever ideas you have about the picture or symbol as well as any personal memories and experiences that are connected with it.

The following are some associations for the four suits of the Tarot cards.

Wands

Phallus symbol, witch's broom, offspring, roots. Stick, material for burning, building material. "Stick jumping out of the bag," drumstick, pointing stick, billiards stick, golf club, tennis racket. Candle, rocket, sun, lightning.

Cups

Trophies, the Holy Grail, the female womb, source, delta. The water of life, fountain of youth, the "broken pitcher." Baptism, tears, drinking, to be left "high and dry." The water reaching up to one's neck, diving under water, letting go of something, swimming free (away from something).

Swords

Tools of war, "swords into plowshares," "He who lives by the sword will die by the sword." Symbol of chivalry, freedom, independence, and maturity. The essence of the power of judgment and ability to make decisions, awareness. Double-edged sword.

Pentacles

Money, talent, everything financial and material. "To coin something" (changing into something else), "to pay back in kind," to shape (mold) and to be shaped. Wealth and poverty, work and harvest. Two sides of a coin. Personal values.

These associations are only examples. Try to bring to each card and each individual symbol your own associations. This does not mean that you should artificially create new or additional meanings for the Tarot symbols. Instead, collect and add your ideas and experiences to each individual symbol when you interpret the cards.

The more of your own impressions and experiences you invest in them, the richer Tarot will be for you. Even individual symbols, like a fish, a snake, a diamond, or a tree, give impetus to many personal memories. And what is true for individual symbols is even truer for each individual card that makes up the whole picture of the Major and Minor Arcana.

Practicing Perception

Describing a Picture Without Judgment

When you are trying to learn about a card, you should do so without judgment. It should be purely an exercise of seeing and describing and, if possible, separate from its explanation and "message." The interpretation takes place afterwards.

Paying Attention

When you first learn about a card, closely and attentively examine the picture and its symbols. What is it that you see in the picture? Are you identifying with the figures in the picture or are you only looking from the perspective of a viewer? Every card is like a puzzle that can be seen differently by different people.

The Tarot Puzzle

This is true for every Tarot card, particularly for the Waite Tarot deck. One of the striking pictures in this deck, which has been often commented on, is the figure of the small woman with the two faces in the "VI-Cups" card. This woman has a double gestalt.

On one hand, she appears to be looking away: her face is colored yellow and framed on the left and right by a reddish-orange scarf.

On the other hand, she can be seen as looking at the figure of a young man: her hair is colored yellow, her face is to the left, and there is a scarf to the right. Both viewpoints are important, but when we look at this card we are, most of the time, only aware of one view: either the face looking away or the face that is looking at the male figure.

Another example is the "VII-Sword" card from the Crowley Tarot deck. It can be seen as if one large sword is holding the other six, as if one major point in an argument is weakening or making less powerful the smaller points. (This can also be a justification for the title of the card, "Futility.")

The same picture can also be described as a large sword absorbing the power of the many smaller ones to gain strength, such as in an argument or intellectual exchange where several opposing opinions are taken into consideration and incorporated into the deliberation. Viewed in this way, the Crowley card with the "seven swords" means something quite different: one large and six smaller swords complement each other and build a pattern like a tree or a clear and beautiful crystal.

Each card should first be examined by what the picture shows. Try to determine how you see the picture. Also, when looking at the picture, try to observe yourself from the outside. What you see is not always obvious because many variations are offered at any given time.

Practicing Interpretation

Interpretation means evaluating and defining your associations and reaction to a specific card in order to understand it. You are working on formulating an idea from what you see and what comes to your mind while temporarily assessing and evaluating what you have experienced in the past.

Interpretation: Evaluate and Define

To expand and improve on the process of interpreting your Tarot cards, remember the following:

• Practice, practice, practice.

• Read, study, and collect already existing theories on interpretation.

• Formulate your own understanding and personal wonder from each card as you look at it.

Just as in dream interpretations, we talk in Tarot about "subjective" and "objective" levels. On the objective level, the varying figures in a picture can stand for other people whom you have met or are going to meet. On the subjective level, the figures are a mirror of some aspect of you.

Subjective and Objective Level

For instance, "VI-The Lovers" card may be seen as your relationship to others as well as to yourself. If you are not quite sure which one it is, work with both possibilities for the time being. "VI-The Lovers" may be depicting you distancing yourself in order to take a critical look at your relationship to others and to yourself.

At the same time, it may be a declaration of love to others as well as to yourself.

Past and Present

The cards always refer to the present time period. The pictures and symbols of Tarot are a mirror for what is now. But while you read the cards, you should be aware of which particular time frame is of interest to you at this moment, because the past and the future are always influencing the present.

We often recognize dangers and problems in a specific picture that hark back to the past. On the other hand, we may encounter unusual, surprising, and astonishing impressions during a reading that could be hinting at unknown possibilities in the future, like a shadow preceding the actual object.

Caution and Encouragement

Every card may indicate that a task has already been accomplished or has yet to be taken on. The message of a card may be a warning, encouragement, or validation. If you are not immediately sure which of these alternatives is the correct one for you at this moment, let all three possibilities be your guide until you reach clarity.

Keep in mind that warnings and encouragements in a card are not mutually exclusive.

Exercises and Practical Consequences

Putting into Action and Testing

The reading and interpretation of a card or layout is only complete if certain practical consequences have been drawn. Try to draw one or several conclusions from every evaluation and interpretation of the symbols. Understand what the card you have pulled means to you and pay attention to how you feel during the process of interpreting it.

Practical Consequences

Everything that you say and do—everything that happens (for instance, getting a telephone call)—while you are questioning Tarot cards can be a part of the message of the respective card. If you keep this in mind, the practical consequences are often right in front of you.

Looking at some cards may cause you to instantaneously sit up, while another card may make you instinctively slump over or feel tired. Your body language is a hint of what the personal meaning of a card may be.

Of course, the practical consequences from card readings can take place on many levels. Let's take two examples. If you pull the "XVI-The Tower" card and choose to act "literally" from your interpretation, you may then decide, for instance, to go parachuting or swimming and diving in a pool. If you choose the "non-literal" consequences, you may see the card as a message to let go of "some much cherished habits" and have the courage to invest yourself wholeheartedly in a subject.

If you take to heart and act on what the "Ace of Cups" might imply, you could take a shower or drink something bubbly. The "non-literal" approach might prod you to openly admit your feelings either to yourself or somebody else, to make peace, to say good-bye, or, in any case, to put a certain experience behind you in order to free yourself.

Of course, there are many other possibilities when it comes to reaching conclusions and making decisions. If at some time you simply cannot understand what the practical consequences of a certain layout are supposed to be, you should accept this as a temporary situation; it is telling you to "tread water," "hang out," or "swim" for a while. However, there is no law that says you cannot reach for another card—even the task is "drawing a practical conclusion."

7. Additional Applications

What Does Tarot Reflect?

Tarot cards reflect everything—every theme, experience, and inquiry—that is put in front of them. In principle, the Tarot will find a connection.

Subjective and Objective Connections

We must differentiate between the subjective and objective connections that Tarot has with other symbolic languages or fields of knowledge.

Objective connections exist between Tarot and the many aspects of fairy tales, mythology, and dreams. We can also make direct connections between Tarot cards and psychological, philosophical, cultural, and historical themes. Tarot's four suits, interpreted as symbols standing for the elements of fire, water, air, and earth, can be linked to the same elements in modern dance that are known as the "four distinct qualities of movement." The same holds true for the connection between Tarot and astrology (starting on page 157).

Tarot and I Ching?

The common aspects of Tarot, I Ching, runes, Qabalah, numerology, certain essential aromas, fragrances, and sounds belong to the subjective side.

In most cases, no factual connections exist between the content of Tarot and, for instance, the I Ching. They are based strictly on purely subjective interpretations. These connections, however, can be effective and meaningful in individual cases although they cannot be generalized.

Tarot and Qabalah?

In 1856, the Qabalah, a part of Jewish mysticism, became connected to the Tarot tradition particularly through the Rosicrucian and theosophy circles. Many different variations of Qabalah interpretation exist.

For instance, every Tarot card is assigned a letter from the Qabalah system and every letter has a numerical value. But opinions vary greatly as to what letter is to be assigned and what numerical value it is to be given. This also applies for the meaning of the Tree of

Life, which is the "road map" of the larger system of Qabalah.

Those who have never heard about Qabalah before do not need to get involved in this subject now, just because they are interested in Tarot. Before 1856, Tarot and Qabalah existed independently for hundreds of years without any direct or indirect connection between them.

Tarot and Numerology?

Be careful when you approach the connection between Tarot and numerology. As in Tarot and Qabalah, every number was given a certain value and meaning in the 19th century. Today, this has changed because of the developments in numerology. Over the years, new questions and ideas have come up.

For instance, which number should be seen as the "holy number"? First, it was the seven, then the eight, then the nine, and finally the number ten. After all this searching, the conclusion is that every number is or could be "holy."

The same holds true for the "Venus Number" as well as for the question: Which numbers are "strong" and which are "weak"? For some people, eleven is the number of "happy beginnings on a higher level." Others consider eleven as the "bad" number.

As a result, the argument over the question whether every number has a certain inherent meaning became absurd. What is accepted is only the general function of numbers (for instance: $3 + 4 = 7$).

More on this subject is discussed in the next chapter.

Tarot Journal

It pays to keep a notebook or a journal so you can keep track of daily spreads, specific interpretations, results, and personal experiences that you have had or are having with the cards. If you want to increase your command of Tarot even more, we recommend that you start a personal Tarot journal.

Read about what the cards may mean to you from different books, but also follow your feelings. What did a card invoke in you independent of any interpretation? Write it all down and, in the end, you will have your very own Tarot book.

Try setting aside two pages for each card. On one page, write the suggestions and interpretations you find from Tarot books while, on the other page, jot down your own personal experiences, dreams, events, etc.

Breathing Exercises and Eye Training

Breathing exercises and training your eyes are particularly useful for deepening and expanding your involvement with Tarot. Many books are available, with practical meditation and visualization techniques.

Tarot and Art

Many writers, musician, painters, and sculptors interpret Tarot cards and have incorporated them into their work. In addition to such well-known people as Italo Calvino and Salvador Dali, a great number of artists and nonartists have developed artistic interpretations of Tarot motifs—in prose and verse, collages and paintings, photo collections and window displays, choreography and musical compositions. There have also been attempts to make Tarot a part of psychodrama and Gestalt psychology.

Tarot Readings in Groups

Tarot cards can be useful in helping to facilitate communication in seminars and consultation sessions. Each member of a group can introduce him/herself with the help of a Tarot card. Or a group can collectively create a story through each member contributing a card. Lining the cards up on the table initiates ideas and becomes a continuing series.

Associative Readings

In an associative reading, you pull the cards without a specific layout in mind. First, think about and make notes on a particular question. Then pull one to three cards. Examine the pictures, decide on their meaning, and expand or moderate your original question. Again, make a note of your findings.

Pull out another one to three cards if you need to expand on the message given on the first round. You may pull these all out at once or one card at a time at each subsequent round. This builds on the card(s) pulled in the previous round and extends on the deliberation of the first stage. For beginners, we recommend pulling only one card each time at each round. Continue this process until you have a satisfying answer.

Here, the design of the layout is less important than your concentrating on the question you have posed and on the attention you give to what you are experiencing at the moment. At the conclusion, you may also calculate the sum-of-the-digit number. Remember that it is the total layout that is providing the answer.

In meditative readings, you choose cards. Be very attentive, relaxed, and concentrate without posing any specific question.

Meditative Reading

Place the deck of cards face up in front of you and examine one card after another. Put aside those cards that "speak" to you and place them in front of you in any manner dictated only by your feelings and intuition.

After you have either gone through the entire deck or decided that you have enough cards, the layout is complete. Breathe consciously and deeply as you take in the whole layout and let the influence the cards have on you sink in.

In Tarot and other symbolic languages, it is important that you keep in mind that the guiding theme is in the transformation or resolution of your personal desires and fears. As long as you make progress, your method of doing Tarot is useful. The opposite is also true. Regardless of how elaborate your knowledge of Tarot reading is and how well you know the language of symbols, if your guiding theme is missing, everything will be worthless for you.

The Guiding Theme

The function of symbols is to build bridges between heaven and earth, between consciousness and unconsciousness. Classical psychotherapy correlates understanding to healing. Building bridges successfully between "below and above" and being fortunate in gaining understanding is the measure of the value that is in the many different uses of Tarot.

8. The Seventy-Eight Cards: A Network

Keep the Numbering in Mind

In contrast to the way numerology was seen in the past, numbers have no specific significance besides their functional value (3 + 4 = 7). This value, however, binds the seventy-eight cards together in a delicate, far-reaching network. But the most important thing to remember is that each Tarot card stands by and for itself.

Significant Connections

Importance of Chronological Order

The chronological order of a card within a suit of the Minor and Major Arcana is instructive. Each card is, in a sense, a mediator. For example, the "V-Cups" is the mediator of "IV-Cups" and "VI-Cups." This gives additional significance to every card.

Organization of the Major Arcana

There are several different opinions about how the twenty-two cards of the Major Arcana are subdivided. One way takes "0-The Fool" card out of the twenty-two-card set. The remaining twenty-one cards are divided into three groups with seven cards each.

The best-known variation is three developmental stages:

First (elementary) stage: I - VII;
Second (spiritual) stage: VIII - XIV;
Third (cosmic) stage: XV - XXI.

The position of the cards in their respective stages corresponds in content to the other cards in their stage: I - VIII - XV; II - IX - XVI; III - X - XVII.

Another commonly used method divides the twenty-one cards into "three ways":

1. The "Osiris Way": I - IV - VII - X - XIII - XVI - XIX.

2. The "Isis Way": II - V - VIII - XI - XIV - XVII - XX.

3. The "Horus Way": III - VI - IX - XII - XV - XVIII - XXI.

According to today's understanding of the Major Arcana, it is important to think of the twenty-two cards as a circle or spiral. They are not only seen as a road or an official opening that quickly gets us from the lower cards (I, II, etc.) to the Major Arcana (XX, 0, and XXI). Rather, they can be experienced again and again, and always at a different stage.

Most of all, the circle makes it possible for each of the twenty-two major cards to become the destination. Therefore, the first cards of the Major Arcana are both an opening for everything that follows as well as the destination.

Additions as an Aid for Interpretation

Looking for additions in cards is helpful in building bridges. If we see the "XVI-The Tower" card as an addition of the VI+X cards (or VII+IX, etc.), we may find more insight into "The Tower," which is not always an easy card to interpret otherwise.

Additions allow us to draw conclusions about a less well known card from two or more well-known ones. Difficult cards are then much easier to read. Their interpretations can then be compared and brought into context. It is also a test as to whether your interpretations are consistent and correspond with each other.

Possibilities with the Major Arcana

In the Major Arcana, the "I-The Magician" card can also be looked at as a 22 + I, the "II-The High Priestess" card as 22 + II, etc. When placed as a circle or spiral, twenty-two is not the final number or the end. For example, XIV + IX = 23 = 22 + I: "Temperance" + "The Hermit" together describe and explain "The Magician." Also, XVII + VII = 24 = 22 + II: "The Star" + "The Chariot" together explain "The High Priestess."

Quintessential Cards

A Quintessential card is the sum of the digits of a complete layout. You can also find the card within the Major Arcana. This represents the conflicting and complementary relationship of the two. For instance, "VI-The Lovers" and "XV-The Devil" represent a conflict and complement. "III-The Empress" and "XII-The Hanged Man" represent a conflict and complement, etc.

Parallel Cards

Parallel cards within the Major Arcana are those with the same final digits: I and XI and XXI, II and XII, III and XIII, IV and XIV, etc. They represent a relation to each other of corresponding ends: base tone and octave, or foreground and background.

For example, "XV-The Devil" represents a more prominent octave or elevated background for "V-The Hierophant." "VII-The Chariot" is the base tone or it stands for the foreground for the higher octave of "XVII-The Star."

Connections Between the Major and Minor Arcana

The Minor Arcana and Its Inner Connections

Numerical values between the suits of the Minor Arcana as well as those between the Major and the Minor Arcana are interconnected. Every card with the same number represents the same theme of the corresponding four elements. This means that whatever effect and meaning the "two of Wands" brings about in the element of fire, it also does the same for the "two of Cups" in the element of water as well as for the "two of Swords" and the "two of Pentacles" in the elements of air and earth, respectively.

The "three of Swords" and the "three of Cups" cards represent the same theme on different levels. The four "X" cards are also equal in their content, even if they are in conflict with how you may have been viewing these cards before. "Ten of Cups" represents just as much good and bad things as the "ten of Pentacles" and "ten of Swords."

Recognizing and Making Use of Connections

The Major Arcana can be seen as a generic term that is expressed on four different levels in the Minor Arcana. For example, the four Minor Cards with the number three have as their superior card the Major Card, "III-The Empress." The Major Card "VII-The Chariot" extensively describes the theme that can be found on different levels in the four Minor Cards with the number seven (VII-Wands, VII-Cups, VII-Swords, and VII-Pentacles).

9. Every Card Is a World by Itself

Because of its different functions—such as additions, Quintessential and parallel cards, the cross-references that are inherent in the symbols—the individual card holds many cross-connections. It is no exaggeration to say that each is a holographic picture that, in a special way, holds all the other seventy-seven cards within it. It therefore makes sense to use the cross-connections that exist for each individual card to accomplish more with Tarot.

Holographic Pictures

It is the task of the beginner to become comfortable with unknown ideas and to gain experience working with them. The advanced reader may find that a certain group of cards is particularly challenging. Doing the different mentioned calculations can serve as a kind of control for blind spots or "fine-tuning" unfamiliar ideas.

Increase Your Intuition

For example, if you see the Waite Tarot cards' "two of Cups" and "three of Cups" as positive while assuming that "five of Cups" represents something negative, you should use the addition method in order to test this assumption. "II-Cups" + "III-Cups" = "V-Cups."

In the Crowley Tarot, the "Ace of Swords" and "VI-Swords" are often welcomed and interpreted as being "good" while the card "VII-Swords" is judged by many to have a stigma attached to it because of its subtitle, "Futility."

The "VII-Swords" is an addition of the cards "Ace of Swords" and "VI-Swords" (or 2 + 5 Swords or 3 + 4 Swords). This can help you clean up any biased interpretations you may have. It can also help you to see the possible dangers and negative aspects you may hold when looking at the "Ace of Swords" and the "VI-Swords" and, likewise, in the positive readings of the "VII-Swords."

**Letting Go of
Projections**

Each card represents a world by itself, and a world for you. Only when blind spots and projections have been removed can you confront the Tarot symbols themselves. Only when the awareness and understanding of the pictures and symbols are not overly influenced by subjective likes and dislikes can you clearly detect your personal desires and fears for what they really are.

If you know and feel in your heart that every one of the seventy-eight cards are absolutely equal, you will more clearly recognize that your present favorite and stress card actually represent your "guiding theme."

Removing projections is one of the principal goals of Tarot readings—going far beyond simply pulling a card for the day or doing a layout. As always, Tarot cards are basically nothing more than a mirror of how you experience and understand your life on a daily basis. By letting go of projections, Tarot readings become a training ground for seeing and appreciating the things in your life, other people as well as yourself, for the way they are.

Practicing Tarot also gives you the opportunity to take apart and reassemble your perceptions, your emotional dispositions, and mental images. With your heart and mind, you are learning to "put yourself together again" in a totally new way.

Chapter 2: Layouts

I. For Every Day

1.
The Card of the Day

1

Reading your card of the day regularly is the most important and wonderful Tarot exercise you can do. It can either be pulled in the morning or evening without generally requiring you to pose a specific question. You should make one card your theme card to specifically highlight a motif for that day.

If possible, find a place for your card so that you can take a quick look at it now and then throughout the day. It is interesting how the significance of the card will grow, how it will come alive, and how it will start to "speak" to you.

This process allows the beginner to become more familiar with the Tarot cards in a theoretical sense as well as to view them as a link to personal and practical events. For the advanced Tarot reader, the card of the day has an even more important meaning. The work with "chance" and the dialogue between the reader and the picture will evolve even more clearly when you ask "How will I view the card that I have pulled?" rather than "What kind of card will I pull?"

A daily card forms a continued involvement. Using Tarot each day for a few minutes will become more rewarding than doing an occasional reading.

2.
Card of the Day Variation

Shuffle the cards. Turn over the top card for your card of the day. Pull out the second card from underneath. This is the background or foundation for the first card.

3.
Card of the Day with Commentary

1 - Card of the day.

2 - Present situation; what is on your mind.

3 - The background for the day's events.

4.
Tasks for the Day

3	2	1

1 - Card of the day.

2 - Specific tasks for the day.

3 - Unique chances during the day.

5.
Today's Choice

1	2

Pull two cards. Disregard one. The other is your card of the day.

6.

The Events of the Day

| 3 | 2 | 1 |

1 - This is the point/this is what's important.

2 - This is how it will evolve.

3 - This is how you begin/this is what you bring to it.

7.

The History of My Day Card

1

Pull a card for the day. Take about 2 minutes to make a note of everything that comes to mind while viewing the card. Remember to see it without any judgments or interpretations.

This is an exercise of association. Write down immediately what you feel and think. You should not take more than 2 minutes. At a later time (maybe in the evening), take another look at the card and your notes.

Examine your card and what came to mind again. Then determine one or two practical consequence(s) to it.

8. & 9.
Two Layouts, Just in Case

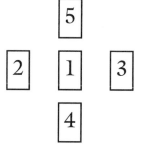

1 - Actual situation.

2 - Past, or how it began.

3 - Future, or what will be new for you.

1 - Key or main aspect.

2 - Past, or how it began.

3 - Future, or what will be new for you.

4 - Root or foundation.

5 - Chance or tendency.

10.
Decision

3

1 2

1 - Situation.

2 - Task.

3 - Decision.

II. Tendencies & Perspectives

11.
The Cross
Variation 1

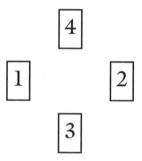

1 - On one hand/the aspects that are already known.

2 - On the other hand/the other side of the coin.

3 - What needs to be changed.

4- The decision, the perspective.

This original layout was created by Oswald Wirth, one of the masters of classical esoteric Tarot interpretation. It is now used in many different variations. Also see Layout #18.

12.
The Cross
Variation 2

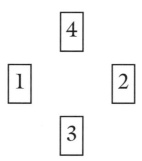

1 and 2 - Main message.

3 - Root or foundation.

4 - Heaven, chance, tendency.

Additional variation: the Quintessential card can be used as a fifth card by being placed in the center. This creates a new picture of the layout. Then another Quintessential card may be calculated using all five cards.

13.
The Cross
Variation 3

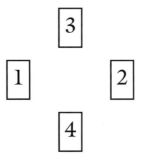

1 - This direction should be avoided.

2 - This is the right direction.

3 - This is the point.

4 - This is where the road will lead to.

14.
The Cross
Variation 4

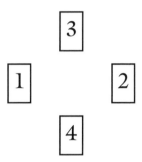

1 - Your theme.

2 - This is your challenge.

3 - This is what you think.

4 - This is what you need.

15.
The Trend
Variation 1

| 1 | 2 | 3 | 4 |

1 - What you already know.

2 - What you are good at.

3 - This is still new.

4 - What you will learn.

16.

The Trend

Variation 2

| 1 | 2 | 3 | 4 | 5 |

1 - What you have.

2 - What you are looking for.

3 - What you should do.

4 - What you want.

5 - What is important for you now.

17.
The Trend
Variation 3

| 1 | 2 | 3 |

1 - What worries you.

2 - What you should not forget.

3 - How you can resolve the situation.

18.

The Cross Road

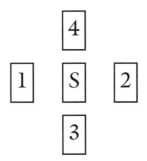

S - The significant theme, the initial question. For this reason, this card is chosen beforehand.

1 - Where does it come from?—describes the origin and foundation of the "S" card.

2 - Where does it lead?—gives information about the direction that "S" will take independently of what you decide to do.

3 - What does this mean for me?—explains the importance of the role and meaning of "S" for you.

4 - What are the possibilities inherent in it or what may open up because of it?—describes what you can achieve because of the encounter with "S."

19.
Checking the Direction of the Trend

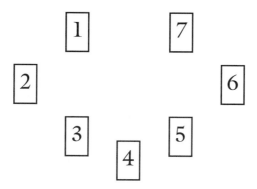

1 - The power of the past.

2 - The power of the present.

3 - The power of the future.

4 and 5 - Suggestions and tips for your behavior.

6 - Obstacles that you must overcome or avoid.

7 - The answer.

20.
Talent and Chance

| 2 | 1 | 3 |

1 - Theme/problem.

2 - Task/challenge.

3 - Chance/talent.

III. Relaxation Exercises

21.
Favorite Card

$$\boxed{1}$$

This card is chosen, not pulled. Ask yourself which of the cards, from what you know and how much you are aware of your feelings about the individual pictures, is your favorite at this particular moment?

Choosing a favorite card from time to time is fun, but this exercise has a deeper meaning. You will be bound to focus on what desires and interests you have at this moment.

22.
The Big Dream

$$\boxed{1}$$

What is the greatest dream or desire you have at this time? Choose a card in the same manner as choosing your favorite card in Layout #21.

23.
"Crazy" Vision

Choose two cards that represent "crazy" ideas and unrealistic fantasies. Look at them.

24.
Tarot Magic

1 - Choose this card. It represents your conscious attitude.

2 - Pull this card. It represents your unconscious attitude.

This layout compares your conscious and unconscious attitudes for a particular subject. First, state your question or subject that you want to find clarity about. Make a note of the question. Then turn the two cards face up and pick the one that draws you the most regarding the question you posed. Next, turn the cards face down again. Shuffle your deck and pull out another card.

25.
Meditative Reading

Try to be attentive, relaxed, and engaging when you choose your cards for a meditative reading. It is not necessary to pose a specific question.

Place the deck of cards face up on the table. Look at each of them one at a time. Pick out those whose pictures seem to catch your attention in a special way and place them in front of you. Without any particular design in mind, create a layout that is only guided by your intuition and feelings.

The layout is complete if you have either gone through the whole deck or simply feel that you have all the cards you want. Take a deep breath, be open to the whole layout, and let it "speak" to you.

26.
Associative Layout

For an associative reading you pull the cards without a specific layout in mind. Think and take notes on a specific question. Then pull anywhere from one to three cards. Examine the pictures and decide on their meaning. Expand or moderate your original question accordingly and, again, make a note of your findings.

Pull out another one to three cards if you need to expand on the message given on the first round. You may either pull out the three new cards at once or one card at a time at each subsequent round. For the beginner, we recommend that you pull one card only at each stage. The card(s) pulled in the previous round will become clearer from the deliberation of the first stage. Continue this process until you have a satisfying answer.

The design of this layout is less important than your concentrating on your question and your paying attention to what you are experiencing at the moment. At the conclusion, you may also calculate the Quintessential card. Remember that the total layout is providing the answer.

27.
Gypsy's Magic Spell

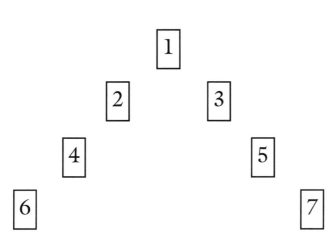

1 - This is you.

2 - This is your defense.

3 - This is what you are afraid of.

4 - This is what drives you.

5 - This is what you are left with.

6 - This is what the future will bring.

7 - This is what brings you back down to the ground.

This is a classic layout that has many different variations.

28.
A Play with Surprises

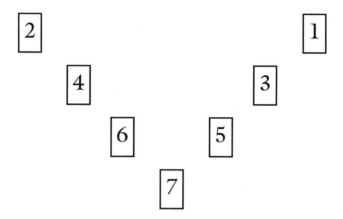

1 - Past I: the known side.

2 - Past II: the unknown side.

3 - Present I: what is here.

4 - Present II: what will come.

5 - Future I: your present plan.

6 - Future II: something unexpected.

7 - Surprise: stunning possibilities.

29.

The Churchyard Spread

1	2	3	4	5	6	7	8	9	10	11	12	13

This layout helps you find the answer to a question and, at the same time, verify it.

Take "0-The Fool" card out of the deck. Shuffle the remaining seventy-seven cards of the deck and place it face down. Pick out twelve cards. Add "The Fool" card, which is also face down, to these twelve cards. Shuffle the thirteen cards again and place them on the table as shown above.

These thirteen cards together are giving you the answer. "0-The Fool" represents the "Zero Hour," the change in the development, or the "Hour of Truth."

Analysis:

(1) "0-The Fool" represents the present. In a way, it is pointing to the direction of the way things are developing. If "The Fool" card is at the beginning of the row, most of what you have to do is still ahead of you; you are at the starting gate. If "The Fool" is near the end, most of what is developing is already behind you.

(2) The position of "The Fool" card within the row also indicates the range of your question. The cards before "The Fool" card indicate what you are consciously aware of. All the cards following "The Fool" describe your unconscious state and an unconscious, or unknown, question that goes beyond your original question.

If "The Fool" card appears at the beginning of the row, most of the aspects concerning your question are either still unknown to you, or the question itself is too narrow in scope. However, if "The Fool" appears at the end of the row, you can be certain that you have a good framework for your question.

If you like, you can may calculate the Quintessential card.

This layout is from Bill Butler's *Dictionary of the Tarot*, New York, 1975, p. 206.

30.
Facing the Gap

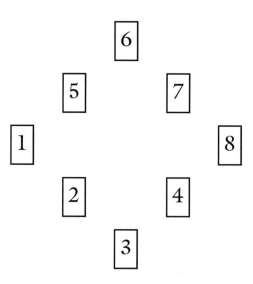

1 - This is possible.

2 - This is important.

3 - This is courageous.

4 - This is futile.

5 - This is necessary.

6 - This is joyful.

7 - This is funny.

8 - This helps you to get ahead.

IV. Concentration & Composure Exercises

31.
In the Blink of an Eye

| 2 | | 1 |

This layout is used to practice concentration and composure when you look at the cards. Take your time so that you can see what you are looking at. Without any particular question in mind, pull out two cards from the deck. Place them on the table face down and mentally prepare yourself to look at the cards for 5 to 10 minutes. Just look and observe what there is to see in each individual card and in both cards together.

Midway through the allotted time, look away from the cards for a few moments. Then look back at the cards for the remainder of the time as if you are seeing them for the first time.

When your time is up, close your eyes for a moment and collect your impressions and associations. You may want to make a few notes. Finish the exercise by thinking about what is expected of you in the day ahead.

32.
Centering

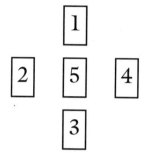

1 - What you see.

2 - What you do.

3 - What you feel and are sensitive to.

4 - What you think.

5 - What/who you are.

33.
Personality Cards

Variation 1: Use your birthday.

Use the numbers of your birthday to calculate the sum-of-the-digit number. For example, August 9, 1963 = 8+9+1+9+6+3 = 36. If this sum falls between 1 and 21, the Major Card of the Tarot deck that has the same number is the personality card. If the calculated number is 22, the card with corresponding number in the Major Arcana is "0-The Fool."

However, if the calculated number is 23 or higher, you have to calculate another sum-of-the-digit number. For instance, the sum-of-the-digit number of 36 is: 3+6 = 9. The Major Card with the corresponding number is then "IX-The Hermit."

Variation 2: Choose one card (see Layout #21).

Variation 3: Pull one card (see Layout #1).

Variation 4: All seventy-eight Tarot cards are a mirror of your personality.

Variation 5: Use the Tarot cards that belong to your specific astrological sign (see pages 166–167).

34.
Stress Card

This card represents the opposite and yet complement to your favorite card (see pages 27 and 63). It is chosen, not pulled.

Which of the cards in the deck appears to be the worst or is the one that makes you the most uncomfortable (from the point of view of what you know about the card and/or how you feel about it)? Which card causes you the most stress when it appears in a layout with both positive or negative meanings?

Each stress card has a corresponding "good luck" card. You need to ask yourself what is so terrible about the stress card. What is the positive side to this stress card? For more information, see pages 27–28.

35.
Hit List

1

2

3

4

5

6

7

8

9

10

These are the ten cards you like the most now.

36.
Anti-Hit List

1

2

3

4

5

6

7

8

9

10

These are the ten cards you like the least now.

37.
The Unknown

1

This card is also chosen. The importance of this exercise rests on your attentiveness, such as in meditative readings (see Layout #25).

Look at each of the Tarot cards and find the one that, at this moment, you seem to know the least about or which represents the unknown to you. Give this card your full attention.

38.
Putting One Card Aside

1

Choose one specific card and put it aside for a future day. Keep it out of sight until the designated time. Do not use this card even in other layouts. Just make a note of which card you have set aside and for how long.

39.
The Four Elements

Look at all four aces of your Tarot card deck. Which of the suit's colors are you most familiar with? Which do you like the best? Which one of the four suits are you most familiar with? Which do you like the least?

40.
Focus of Attention

This is an exercise where you use only the Court Cards (Queen, King, Knight, and Page). Place all of them in front of you. Relax and concentrate on the pictures. Pick out the card that is making the greatest impression on you—positive or negative. Take a few minutes to observe and make notes, beginning with the sentence "My relationship to this card is . . ."

When you are done, change the sentence to: "My relationship to myself is . . ." and read your notes again.

V. Searching & Finding

41.
The Star

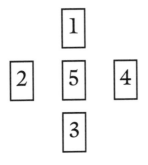

1 - Where you are.

2 - Your task.

3 - Your difficulties.

4 - Your strengths.

5 - Your goal.

42.
The Pentagram

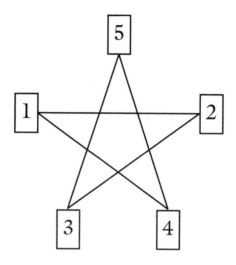

1 - This is where you came from.

2 - This is where you are going.

3 - This is what is difficult for you.

4 - This is what makes sense.

5 - This is your ultimate goal.

43.
Separating & Bonding

1 - This is what I will be rid of.

2 - This is what I will take care of.

3 - This is what I will accomplish.

44.
The Question Game

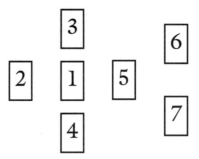

1 - My situation/my problem.

2 - This is how it happened.

3 - This is the way I feel today.

4 - This is what I am afraid of.

5 - This will happen in the future.

6 - This is the warning the Tarot cards are sending.

7 - This is the suggestion the Tarot cards are sending.

45.
Desires & Fears

| 1 | 2 |
| 4 | 3 |

1 - This will get me ahead.

2 - This will set me back.

3 - This is misleading me.

4 - This promises good luck.

46.
New Answers

1 - This you know.

2 - This new arrival is near.

This layout may be used several times in a row.
For instance:

(1) Concerning relationships and partnerships.

(2) At work.

(3) At home.

47.

The Path or Turning Point

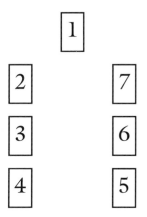

1 - This is the point. These are the chances and risks concerning this question.

The left column represents your conduct up until now:

2 - Conscious attitude and rational behavior. Thought, logical reasoning, intentions, conduct. What you think and have been thinking.

3 - Unconscious belief and emotional reasoning. Wishes, desires, hopes, and fears. What you feel or have been feeling.

4 - Outward appearance. How you present yourself, how you affect others and, in turn, the facade you present.

The right column represents suggestions for how to conduct yourself in the future (interpretations corresponding to the cards 2 to 4):

7 - Conscious attitude. Suggestions for rational approach.

6 - Unconscious conduct. Suggestions concerning emotional attitude.

5 - Outward appearance. This is how you should conduct yourself. You should do and acknowledge this.

48.
New Values
Variation 1

```
┌───┐
│ 3 │
└───┘
        ┌───┐
        │ 2 │
        └───┘
                ┌───┐
                │ 1 │
                └───┘
```

Variation 2

```
                ┌───┐
                │ 1 │
                └───┘
        ┌───┐
        │ 2 │
        └───┘
┌───┐
│ 3 │
└───┘
```

1 - This will become less important.

2 - This will become more important.

3 - This is now essential.

49.
Finding the Goal

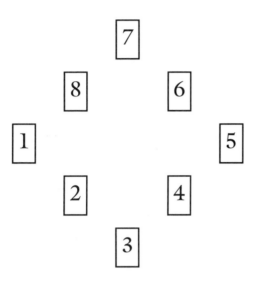

1 - Your starting point.

2 - Your strengths and skills.

3 - This is an old problem for you.

4 - Your weaknesses/your vices.

5 - New starting point/influences of other/your other side.

6 - Unknown talents.

7 - New kinds of chances.

8 - Proof that your passions are worthwhile.

9 (= Card 1) - New tasks/new goal.

50.
Know Thyself

1 - Who am I?

2 - What are my needs?

3 - How do I go about meeting my needs?

51.
This Is Also Who I Am

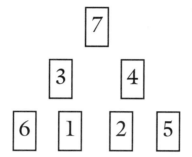

1 - How I feel.

2 - What I know.

3 - What I believe . . .

4 - . . . and what I will hold on to.

5 - What I don't know . . .

6 - . . . maybe just suspect.

7 - This is also who I am.

52.
Blind Spot

- Discovering your blind spots is not a sign of weakness. On the contrary, it addresses your personal strengths.

- Tarot cards do not "invent" blind spots. They only mirror the way we see the things that follow us daily. Finding a blind spot is of value to everything that concerns our life.

- Cards used to discover blind spots can neither be chosen nor pulled. We would then only see what we already know—not what we don't—which is precisely the "blind spot in the lens."

- The best sign of a blind spot is when you look at a card and think that the person who has painted the picture has made a mistake.

- Cards that you perceive as being either exclusively positive or negative are also the clearest indicators of blind spots.

53.
Inner Strength

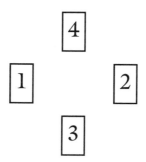

1 - My responsibilities.

2 - What I love.

3 - What my inner voice is telling me.

4 - My decision.

54.
What Is the Cause of My . . . ?*
Variation 1

1- From here on.

55.
What Is the Cause of My . . . ?*
Variation 2

| 1 | 2 | 3 |

1 - From here on.

2 - But also from here on.

3 - And absolutely from here on.

* Depending on your present situation, replace the ellipses of the layout title with joy, sadness, anger, longing, etc.

56.
Where and How Do I Find . . . ?

1

1 - The answer.

57.
How Do I Find . . . ?

1   2

1 - This way.

2 - And this way.

58.
Where Do I Find . . . ?

| 1 | 2 |

1 - Not here.

2 - But here.

59.
Stages of Change 1

| 1 | 2 | 3 | 4 | 5 |

1 - This is over and done with.

2 - This is over but the effects linger on.

3 - This is where I am heading.

4 - This is what I expect.

5 - This is what I am supposed to learn right now.

60.
Stages of Change 2

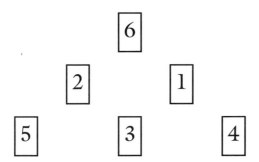

1 - This is what I want.

2 - I don't like this, but that's the way it is.

3 - This is what A wants (e.g., a partner).

4 - This is what B wants (e.g., children or friends).

5 - This is what C wants (e.g., a colleague or neighbor).

6 - This is the best thing for everybody involved.

61.
Stages of Change 3

```
┌───┐   ┌───┐
│ 1 │   │ 2 │
└───┘   └───┘
┌───┐   ┌───┐
│ 3 │   │ 4 │
└───┘   └───┘
```

1 - A fear that is dissipating.

2 - A wish that has been fulfilled.

3 - A force that is carrying me.

4 - A longing that stays with me.

62.
The Path of Desires

| 1 | | 3 | | 4 | | 5 | | 2 |

These cards are chosen, not pulled, for this layout. The first card represents what is. Relax, concentrate, and choose a card that fits your present situation. Place it in front of you. Next, find a card for what should be—meaning what you desire. Take as much time as you need.

Once you have found and placed these cards on the table, spread them apart and pick three more cards to serve as the connection or bridge to help you get from what is to the desired goal. Make sure that the three cards you pick for the bridge are able to "carry the weight" of getting you to the other side. In the end, look at the whole row as one path and one event (Quintessential card).

1 - Present situation.

2 - What you desire.

3, 4, and 5 - Bridge between Cards 1 and 2.

VI. Questions About Decisions

63.
Decision

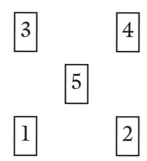

1 and 2 - Where you came from.

3 and 4 - Where you are headed to, including the dangers/chances.

1 and 3 - This speaks against it.

2 and 4 - This speaks in favor of it.

5 - The decision.

64.

The Reasons for the Decision

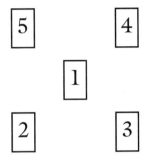

1 - Key or main aspect.

2 - This is what drives you.

3 - Outside influences.

4 - Danger or risk.

5 - This is how it will work out.

65.
Immediate Consequences

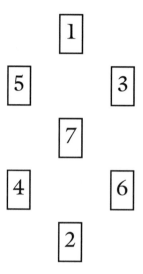

1 - Your strengths.

2 - Your weaknesses.

3 - Assistance.

4 - Resistance.

5 - This is the decision you should make.

6 - This is what will then happen.

7 - Your solution.

66.
Naming the Problem

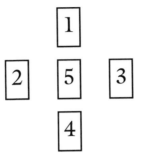

1 - My problem/the subject.

2 - This is what I can't change.

3 - This is what I can change/do.

4 - What other alternatives are open to me.

5 - Quintessential card; how things will progress for now.

67.
The Solution

1 - The task.

2 - The problem that is connected to it.

3 - The solution.

4 - New insights.

5 - The conclusion.

68.
The Essentials

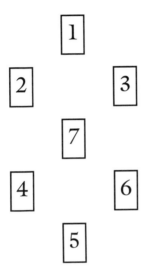

1 - Your opinion.

2 - What you see clearly.

3 - What you forget easily.

4 - The opinions of others.

5 - What others are seeing clearly.

6 - What others easily overlook.

7 - What is essential.

69.
Prioritizing

```
┌───┐   ┌───┐
│ 2 │   │ 1 │
└───┘   └───┘
```

1 - This is what I will do now.

2 - This I will accomplish later.

70.
The Next Step

1

1 - This is what I will concentrate on now.

71.
The Next Steps

| 2 | 1 | 3 |

1 - This is important now.

2 - I will set this aside for now.

3 - This is what I have to take into consideration.

72.
The Sword

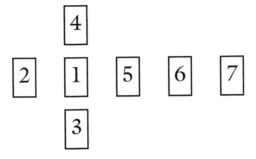

1 - The heart of the matter.

2 - Your starting point.

3 - Your base or support.

4 - Your chance/what will aid you.

5 - A problem is being solved.

6 - A desire is being fulfilled.

7 - New knowledge, new insight.

VII. Partnership & Relationships

73.
Joint Solution

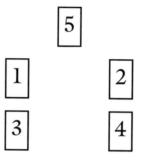

1 - My partner.

2 - Myself.

3 - This is what's important to him/her.

4 - This is what's important to me.

5 - The joint solution.

74.
Partnership

3

1   2

1 - My partner.

2 - Myself.

3 - The joint tasks or chances.

75.
Partnership Tarot

| 1 | 3 | 5 |
| 2 | 4 | 6 |

1 - Partner A pulls a card for Partner B: This how I see you.

2 - Partner B pulls a card for Partner A: This how I see you.

3 - Partner A pulls a card for him/herself: This is how I see myself.

4 - Partner B pulls a card for him/herself: This is how I see myself.

5 - Partner A pulls a card that shows his/her relationship to Partner B.

6 - Partner B pulls a card that shows his/her relationship to Partner A.

Turn each card face up one at a time. Pay attention to your initial reactions as you say to your partner: "With this card, I say to you . . . "; or "I am getting from you . . . "; or "I give you at this moment . . . "

76.
Partnership as Mirror

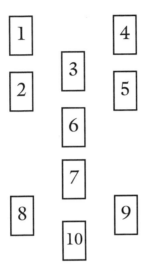

1 - Myself.

2 - How do I see my partner?

3 - How do I see our relationship?

4 - This will strengthen our relationship.

5 - This will weaken our relationship.

6 - My hopes.

7 - My fears.

8 - My responsibility in this relationship.

9 - My partner's responsibility in this relationship.

10 - This is what will happen.

77.
Relationships

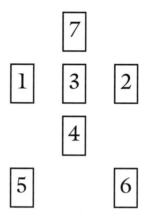

1 - My partner.

2 - Myself.

3 - The power that connects us.

4 - Our common base.

5 - The resources of my partner.

6 - My resources.

7 - The focal point. Our mutual goal.

78.

Tarot Encounter

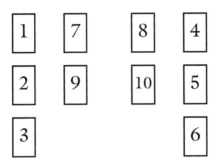

If you want to do a reading for two people who are looking to clarify their relationship, have Partner A pull Cards 1 to 3 and Partner B pull Cards 4 to 6.

Cards 1 and 4 represent the head; Cards 2 and 5, the heart; Cards 3 and 6, the belly.

Discuss with each partner what the cards are saying. Make sure that Partner B is only listening and does not becomes involved with your discussion of Partner A's interpretation, and vice versa. Consult the cards about how and on what level both partners are agreeing and where they have problems.

Next, have Partner A pull a card that represents what he/she wants to say to Partner B (Card 7). Formulate the message while Partner B only watches. Then, have Partner B pull Card 8 and Partner A must remain silent.

Continue in this manner for Cards 9 and 10, until both partners can see each other's needs and accept them openly without judgment.

79.
I Love Them All . . .

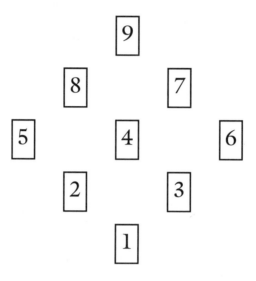

1 - The child . . .

2 - The angel . . .

3 - The devil . . .

4 - The nameless . . .

5 - The feminine . . .

6 - The masculine . . .

7 - The special . . .

8 - The insignificant . . .

9 - The mature . . .

. . . person in me.

80.
The Three Desires

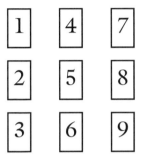

1 - My love.

2 - My cravings.

3 - My passion.

4 - Your love.

5 - Your cravings.

6 - Your passion.

7 - Quintessential card of Cards 1 + 4. Our love.

8 - Quintessential card of Cards 2 + 5. Our cravings.

9 - Quintessential card of Cards 3 + 6. Our passion.

81.
I Love Because . . .

1

1 - The answer.

82.
Testing Love

	1	
2	5	4
	3	

1 - What my love relationship means to me at this time.

2 - What I really love about it.

3 - What I don't like about it.

4 - What gives new energy (and wings) to love.

5 - What I still don't know about love and what I will now learn.

VIII. Life Journey

83.
Inventory

1	2	3	Past
6	5	4	Present
7	8	9	Future

84.
Setting a Goal

1

4

3   2

1 - My goal.

2 - Which qualities of mine will help me reach my goal?

3 - Which shortcomings keep me from reaching my goal?

4 - How can I reach my goal?

85.
The Road to the Solution

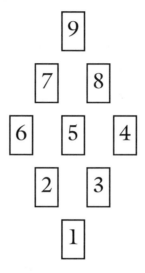

1 - Your dowry.

2 - . . . its curse.

3 - . . . its promise.

4 - A challenge for you.

5 - This will remain a puzzle to you.

6 - This is a necessary burden for you.

7 - Your task.

8 - Your problem.

9 - The solution.

86.
Ultimate Happiness

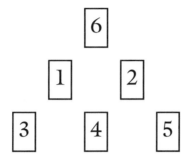

1 - This is what you will get rid of.

2 - This is what you will accomplish.

3 - This goes with it.

4 - This will bring you luck.

5 - You will still be confronted with this.

6 - This solution as a blessing.

87.
Present and Future

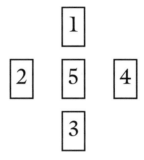

1 - Where you stand.

2 - Your task.

3 - Your fears.

4 - Which attitude will help you get ahead.

5 - The outcome of your efforts.

88.
Path and Goal

| 1 | 3 | 2 |

These cards are chosen from the twenty-two cards of the Major Arcana:

1 - Where you stand now.

2 - Where you want to be (your goal).

3 - Your path.

The third card is determined by the number of steps it takes to get from 1 to 2 within the circle of the twenty-two Major Cards. For example: 1 = IX-The Hermit; 2 = XIX-The Sun; 3 = X-Wheel of Fortune (the path from IX to XIX). Or: 1 = XXI-The World; 2 = VI-The Lovers; 3 = VII-The Chariot.

89.
Progress Cards

7	8	9
4	5	6
1	2	3

1, 2, 3 - Love.

4, 5, 6 - Creativity.

7, 8, 9 - Calling.

90.
Self-Definition

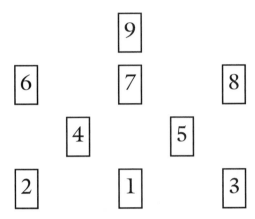

1 - I am . . .

2 - I am not . . .

3 - I am also . . .

4 - What I can't understand about myself . . .

5 - What I am really proud of myself for . . .

6 - The worst that anybody can say to me . . .

7 - The most wonderful thing that somebody can say to me . . .

8 - The most honest thing that somebody can say about me . . .

9 - In one word . . .

91.
Homework

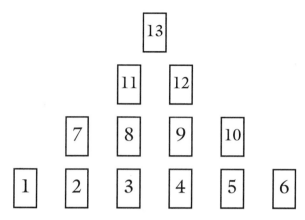

1 - What did I learn?

2 - What can I rely on?

3 - Which fruits are ripe now?

4 - What results are still missing?

5 - Which one of my aspirations gives me strength?

6 - And which one weakens me?

7 - What fears will I confront?

8 - And which ones should I leave alone?

9 - Which one of my goals has proven to be positive?

10 - What is it that holds me back?

11 - What does not suit me?

12 - Where do I find support?

13 - How can I emphasize my wishes?

92.
Dream Goal

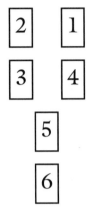

1 - Where I stand.

2 - Where I am going.

3 - My aspiration.

4 - My fears.

5 - My true desire.

6 - The secret of the search.

IX. Preview & Overview

93.
The Cycle of the Year
Variation 1

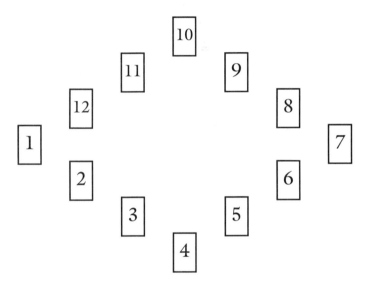

1 - The Aries in me: What I am and how I am.
2 - The Taurus in me: What I have and how I own it.
3 - The Gemini in me: What I think and how I think.
4 - The Cancer in me: What I feel and how I feel it.
5 - The Leo in me: What I desire and how I choose it.
6 - The Virgo in me: What I analyze and how I resolve it.
7 - The Libra in me: What I balance and how I balance it.
8 - The Scorpio in me: What I demand and how I demand it.
9 - The Sagittarius in me: What I see and how I see it.
10 - The Capricorn in me: What I gain and how I benefit from it.
11 - The Aquarius in me: What I know and how I know it.
12 - The Pisces in me: What I believe and how I believe it.

94.
The Cycle of the Year
Variation 2

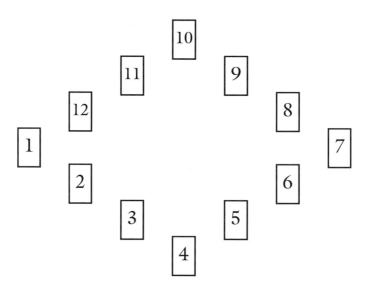

1 - Your possibilities and intentions.

2 - Your financial situation: Acquisition.

3 - Your nearby environment: Family members. News of the day. Small changes (in location). Brothers and sisters.

4 - Marriage. Family. Father.

5 - Your emotional life: Works and creations. Children.

6 - Work. Health.

7 - Your external world: Connections and associations. Marriage. The couple.

8 - Changes. Rewards. Profound changes.

9 - Your intellectual life. Travels. Higher education. Management.

10 - Social ambitions. The Ideal. Mother.

11 - Your connections and support: Plans. Hopes.

12 - Probing. Struggles. Secret things.

At the end, we recommend you calculate the Quintessential card.

95.
The Cycle of the Year
Variation 3

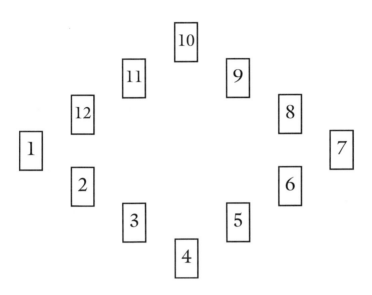

1 - Who am I? (personal attributes, character)
2 - How attached am I? (possessions, locality)
3 - How easy is it for me to get on? (in the environment, social circles, communication)
4 - How do I feel? (emotional life, relationship to mother, the feminine)
5 - How do I express myself? (expressiveness, relationship to father, the masculine)
6 - How do I adapt? (concerning my surroundings)
7 - How do I approach others? (relationships, community)
8 - What are my guides? (my heroes, ideas)
9 - How do I determine? (world attitudes, worldview, giving meaning)
10 - What do I create? (work, profession)
11 - What sets me free? (living life successfully, support from friends)
12 - What fulfills me? (spirituality, transcendence)

96.
The Cycle of the Year
Variation 4

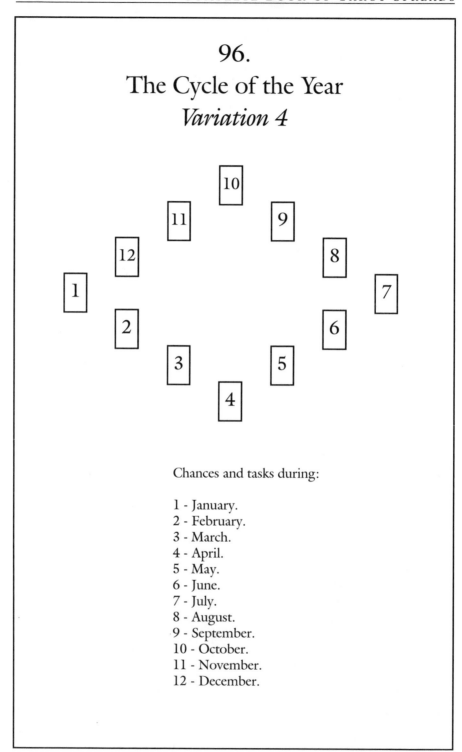

Chances and tasks during:

1 - January.
2 - February.
3 - March.
4 - April.
5 - May.
6 - June.
7 - July.
8 - August.
9 - September.
10 - October.
11 - November.
12 - December.

97.
Additional Year Card

Variation 1: Pull cards for the layout of your choice.

Variation 2: Choose cards for the layout of your choice.

Variation 3: Calculate cards (see page 21).

98.
Tarot Table

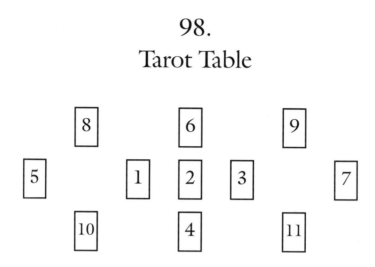

The first three cards present the essence of the question.

1 - The questioner; subject of the question; theme; significant factor.

2 - Cover card; that which directly touches the questioner.

3 - Opposing or complementary card.

4 - Present situation; situation at the time the question is posed.

5 - Root, past; basis from which the question arose.

6 - Immediate future; next prospect.

7 - Expectation, further development; taking all cards in the layout into consideration.

8 - Yourself, inner strength, inner depth, the unconscious.

9 - Hopes and fears; feelings about the question.

10 - Surroundings and influences from the outside.

11 - The energies that you are aware of already being in effect because, in the context of your question, they are becoming increasingly more important.

99.
The Celtic or Sun Cross
Variation 1

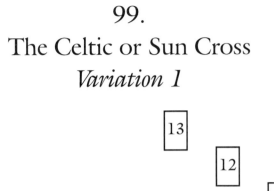
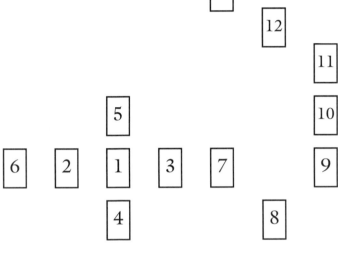

1 - You and the argument in question.
2 - Positive addition to 1.
3 - Negative addition to 1.
4 - Root, basis, support.
5 - Culmination, chance, tendency.
6 - The past, or what is happening now.
7 - The future, or what is new and has to be taken into consideration.
8 - Summary of positions 1–7; your inner strength, your unconscious.
9 - Your hopes and fears.
10 - Surroundings and influences from the outside, your external face.
11, 12, 13 - Summation, or a factor you are made aware of specifically because, in the context of your question, it is becoming increasingly more important.

100.
The Celtic or Sun Cross
Variation 2

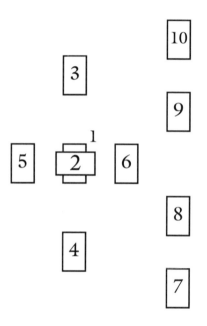

1 - What envelops and surrounds you (or your question).
2 - What crucifies you.
3 - What completes you.
4 - What lies underneath you.
5 - What is behind you.
6 - What lies ahead of you.
7 - This is you.
8 - What surrounds you.
9 - Your hopes and fears.
10 - What will come to you.

101.
The Celtic or Sun Cross
Variation 3

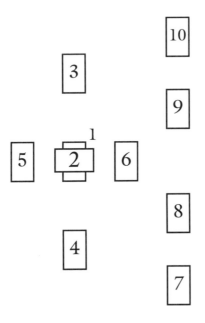

1 - Starting point.
2 - Cross card, opposing or complementary to 1.
3 - Chances, culmination, conscious side.
4 - Root, basis, unconscious side.
5 - Past.
6 - Future.
7 - Inner strength, inner attitude.
8 - Hopes and fears.
9 - Outside influences and the attitude you present to the world.
10 - Outcome, goal, task.

102.
The Celtic or Sun Cross
Variation 4

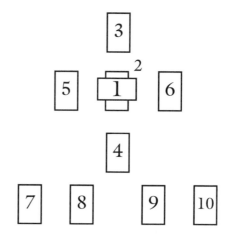

1 - Starting point.

2 - Cross card, opposing or complementary to 1.

3 - Chances, culmination, conscious side.

4 - Root, basis, unconscious side.

5 - Past.

6 - Future.

7 - Inner strength, inner attitude.

8 - Hopes and fears.

9 - Outside influences and the attitude you present to the world.

10 - Outcome, goal, task.

X. Major Layouts

103.
Gypsy-Method
Variation 1

	A	B	C	D	E	F	G
III	15	16	17	18	19	20	21
II	8	9	10	11	12	13	14
I	1	2	3	4	5	6	7

I - Past.
II - Present.
III - Future.

A - Work and success.
B - Plans and intentions.
C - Lucky and unlucky.
D - Friends and support.
E - Love and erotica.
F - Family.
G - Personal state (of health, affairs, etc.).

104.
Gypsy Method
Variation 2

The twenty-one cards that you pull from the deck can be placed either face up or, for the time being, face down. If faced down, turn them over and read each card one at a time.

G	F	E	D	C	B	A
7	6	5	4	3	2	1
14	13	12	11	10	9	8
21	20	19	18	17	16	15

The numbers in each column represent one continuous picture. The columns have the following meaning:

A - Your emotional state of mind.

B - Your home life.

C - Your present desires, hopes, and questions.

D - Your expectations of the situation.

E - What you do not expect, what surprises you.

F - Your immediate future.

G - The outcome and long-term prospects.

105.
Pyramid
Variation 1

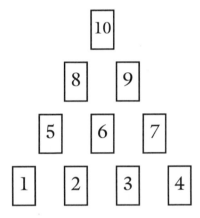

1, 2, 3, 4 - Past.

5, 6, 7 - Present.

8, 9 - Future.

10 - Outcome.

106.
Pyramid
Variation 2

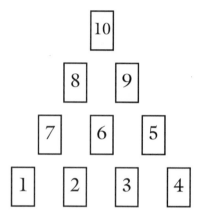

1, 2, 3, 4 - Task.

5, 6, 7 - Obstacles.

8, 9 - Help/solution.

10 - The outcome of your efforts.

107.
Turning Point

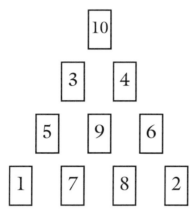

1 - Root/culmination.
2 - Fear/security.
3 - Trauma/rescue.
4 - Point of escaping.
5 - Pain/relief from grief.
6 - Joy/great fortune.
7 - Test/completion.
8 - Foreign land/at home.
9 - Unrest/clarification.
10 - Major gamble/major task.

This layout "flourishes" on the double meaning in each card. For instance, the description of position 4, "the point of escaping," implies that we are escaping from something as well as toward something (it could be the same point, but also a totally different one). Every position in the layout has a similar double entendre.

108.
Tarot Table 2

| 12 | 14 | 16 | 18 | 20 |

| 11 | 13 | 15 | 17 | 19 |

| S |

| 1 | 3 | 5 | 7 | 9 |

| 2 | 4 | 6 | 8 | 10 |

S - Significant factor.

1, 2 - The situation of the questioner (relating to the material aspect); how the questioner understands and feels about it.

3, 4 - The surroundings, the situation of the questioner (family, friends, etc.).

5, 6 - Intention or what the questioner is trying to achieve, to attain, or has planned.

7, 8 - Influences that could work against what the questioner is intending to do.

9, 10 - Possible losses or limits that could hinder the questioner.

11, 12 - The activities of the questioner; what he/she is undertaking or trying to realize.

13, 14 - Desires, hopes, or fears the questioner may have that stir his/her imagination.

15, 16 - The expectations of the questioner from what he/she believes (based on how his/her present situation is evaluated) will be confronted in the near future.

17, 18 - The immediate future, what will happen next, and the meaning it has for the questioner.

19, 20 - Influences that will have long-tern implications for the questioner and, thereby, are an indication of the direction that the events in his/her life will take.

109.
The Fan

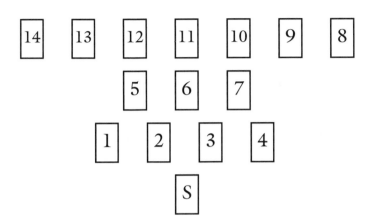

S - The significant card, indicating the initial question if it is taken out beforehand. Otherwise, this card represents the theme of the layout. In either case, the card is part of the layout.

Cards 2, 3, 6, and 11 refer to the transition from the past to the future and describe the events of the present situation.

Cards 1, 5, 12, 13, and 14 show the influences of the past that continue to be relevant for the questioner.

Cards 4, 7, 8, 9, and 10 refer to the future, future events, and the path ahead.

110.
Golden Dawn Divination

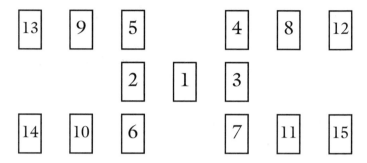

1 - This card symbolizes the questioner, his/her problems, present situation, and main influences. A Court Card (Queen, King, Prince, or Page) in this position represents either the questioner or any other important person (if the gender of the card is the opposite of the questioner). A Court Card of the same gender that does not resemble the questioner can also have a significant influence on the life of the questioner.

2 and 3 - Together with Card 1, these two cards give extensive information about the situation and the personality of the questioner.

4, 8, and 12 - These cards show the direction that the life of the questioner will naturally take, as long as nothing is attempted to alter it ("The stars are urging, but not the force").

13, 9, and 5 - These show the possibilities to act differently, which may be desirable or detrimental, depending on the rest of the cards.

14, 10, and 6 - These cards help the questioner make the necessary decisions. For the older reader, these cards represent past actions and events that are influencing the question. For the younger reader, they give an indication of the future.

7, 11, and 15 - These cards show powers that are beyond the control of the questioner. You cannot change them. You can only adapt to them.

111.
Tarot Table 3

			1			
F 37	38	39	40	41	42	43
E 30	31	32	33	34	35	36
D 23	24	25	26	27	28	29
C 16	17	18	19	20	21	22
B 9	10	11	12	13	14	15
A 2	3	4	5	6	7	8

1 - Personality card (may be either pulled or chosen).

A - Past.

B - Present.

C - Future.

D - Actual influences.

E - Future possibilities/chances for growth.

F - Life's goals and tasks.

XI. Departures

112.
Turning Back

2

1

1 - What I regret/what I will do differently now.

2 - This helps in doing it.

113.
Good-bye 1

2	1	3

1 - The situation/the good-bye.

2 - What I will let go of.

3 - The next step.

114.
Good-bye 2

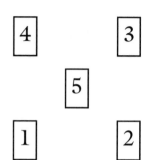

1 - This is what I originally wanted.

2 - How it is now.

3 - What I am saying good-bye to.

4 - What remains behind.

5 - How it will be from here.

115.
Good-bye 3

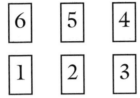

1 - My anger.

2 - My sadness.

3 - My powerlessness.

4 - My desire.

5 - My search.

6 - My support.

116.
Letting Go in Order to Gain

1 - What I will let go of.

2 - What I will gain (accomplish, realize).

117.
Damned . . .

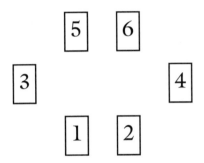

1 - This scares me.

2 - This fascinates me.

3 - This is what I can do without.

4 - I have some catching up to do here.

5 - This is what I refuse.

6 - This is what I will get used to.

118.
My Greatest Vice

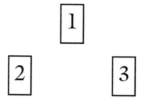

1 - Vice/weakness/what I have a weakness for.

2 - This is what drags me down.

3 - This gives me a cause.

119.
My Greatest Strength

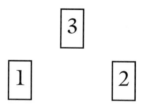

1 - This will not leave me in peace.

2 - This gives me form.

3 - My strengths/my virtues.

120.
My Most Important Talent

1

1 - Current answer.

121.
My Favorite Layout

Choose your favorite layout or construct your own.

122.
Very Personal

This layout addresses the question "What I always wanted to know about myself and what nobody can tell me."

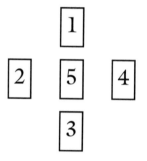

1 - Where I stand.

2 - My tasks.

3 - My fears.

4 - Which attitude will help me along.

5 - The outcome of my efforts.

Chapter 3: Tarot and Astrology

The interconnections of Tarot and astrology lead to interesting perspectives; you can literally see the images of astrological concepts and ideas, which gives an additional dimension to the meaning of each individual Tarot card. Combining the symbolic language of Tarot and astrology is a rather new phenomenon. About 100 years ago, the Golden Dawn Order developed a systematic model that formed this logical coming together.

Visual Concepts

The Golden Dawn Order was a Rosicrucian association in England devoted to occult studies. It was founded in 1888 but disbanded soon after 1910. The order tried to consolidate a variety of rich, esoteric 19th century theories, and Tarot cards played a part in its attempts.

The Golden Dawn Order

Today's most commonly used Tarot decks were created by former members of the Golden Dawn Order: Pamela Colman Smith and Arthur A. Waite, as well as Lady Frieda Harris and Aleister Crowley. Without the Rider-Waite and Crowley Tarot decks, the rise in interest of Tarot in the last 10 to 20 years would be unthinkable.

Pamela Colman Smith and Arthur A. Waite, Lady Frieda Harris and Aleister Crowley

In the conception of their cards, Smith/Waite and Harris/Crowley faithfully adhered, with only minor differences, to the astrological classification that the Golden Dawn Order developed. In the Waite Tarot cards, you will find Aries in the "IV-The Emperor" card, Taurus in the "King of the Pentacles" card, etc. In the Crowley Tarot deck, almost all of the astrological signs have been incorporated.

The symbolic languages of Tarot and astrology have their own life, and when you view them as such you will then find meaningful connections. Tarot pictures would wither if you only used them as allegories or as illustrations of astrological philosophy. Astrological interpretations would diminish if they were used only as a supplement to Tarot symbols. Each symbolic language has its own logic, its own kind of awareness. The clearer their differences, the richer will be their common ground.

Each Symbolic Language Has Its Own Logic

The following are the major points of reference on the connections between Tarot and astrology.

Definition of Astrological Signs

Aries: I am
Taurus: I have
Gemini: I think
Cancer: I feel
Leo: I want
Virgo: I analyze
Libra: I balance
Scorpio: I desire
Sagittarius: I see
Capricorn: I use
Aquarius: I know
Pisces: I believe

These definitions are accepted by almost all astrological orders.

Major Arcana and the Astrological Signs

Aries: IV-The Emperor
Taurus: V-The Hierophant
Gemini: VI-The Lovers
Cancer: VII-The Chariot
Leo: VIII/XI-Strength (Lust)
Virgo: IX-The Hermit
Libra: XI/VIII-Justice (Adjustment)
Scorpio: XIII-Death
Sagittarius: XIV-Temperance (Art)
Capricorn: XV-The Devil
Aquarius: XVII-The Star
Pisces: XVIII-The Moon

The names in parenthesis are used in the Crowley Tarot cards. The Golden Dawn Order originally transposed the Major Cards VIII and XI, which since has been adapted by many other Tarot variations, such as the Waite Tarot.

Traditionally, in the Major Cards, VIII = Strength and XI = Justice. The transposition makes VIII = Strength (Lust) and XI = Justice (Adjustment). If you calculate a sum-of-the-digit or determine a lucky card, it makes a difference which numbers are chosen for Leo and Libra.

The question regarding which variation is "correct" has been the subject of, at times, fierce but always futile debate. We recommend you follow the sequence of numbers that is being used in your Tarot deck.

Court Cards and the Astrological Signs

Aries: Queen of Wands
Taurus: King of Pentacles (Prince of Disks)
Gemini: Knight of Swords
Cancer: Queen of Cups
Leo: King of Wands (Prince of Wands)
Virgo: Knight of Pentacles (Knight of Disks)
Libra: Queen of Swords
Scorpio: King of Cups (Prince of Cups)
Sagittarius: Knight of Wands
Capricorn: Queen of Pentacles (Queen of Disks)
Aquarius: King of Swords (Prince of Swords)
Pisces: Knight of Cups

The names in parentheses above are titles used in the Crowley Tarot.

Crowley's Court Cards: The Difference

The method used to organize the Court Cards in the Crowley Tarot deck is not obvious. Normally, we have the Queen, King, Knight, and Page. In the Crowley deck, the Court Cards are: Queen, Prince, Knight, and Princess.

To which Court Cards in the commonly used Tarot deck do the Court Cards in the Crowley Tarot correspond?

Crowley, in the book that accompanies the cards he designed, gives a rather ambiguous answer. On the one hand, he describes the Knight as being the strongest and most powerful of the four Court Cards. This would therefore mean that Crowley's Knight corresponds to the King in the other Tarot decks.

On the other hand, Crowley has supplied a specific astrological constellation for every card. His pictures are full of, even steeped in, astrological symbols and concepts. For instance, "VII-The Chariot" is specifically assigned to the sign of Cancer, underscoring the fact that both Neptune and Jupiter are elevated for this astrological sign.

According to Crowley's own explanation, astrology plays a prominent role in his version of Tarot, and the astrological descriptions and organizations, which he himself assigned to his Court Cards, correspond to the Waite and Marseille Tarot:

Waite and Marseille Tarot	Crowley Tarot
Queen	Queen
King	Prince
Knight	Knight
Page	Princess

From an astrological point of view, the Waite, Marseille, and Crowley Tarot decks seem to be clear: the Knight in the Crowley deck corresponds to the Knight in all the other versions of Tarot, the Prince in the Crowley deck to the King in all the others.

In general, Crowley's definition of the Court Cards is not clearly stated, and that was his intention. He wanted to introduce a system that was different from all the others. For that reason, Crowley's comments allow you to come to different conclusions.

Cards for the Astrological "Planets"

Ten "Planets"   In astrology, the sun and moon are considered planets. The list of planets is presented from the center of our solar system outward. Our planet earth has been omitted here.

Sun: XIX-The Sun
Mercury: I-The Magician

Venus: III-The Empress
Moon: II-The High Priestess (The Priestess)
Mars: XVI-The Tower
Jupiter: X-The Wheel of Fortune (Fortune)
Saturn: XXI-The World (The Universe)
Uranus: XXII/0-The Fool
Neptune: XII-The Hanged Man
Pluto: XX-Judgment (The Aeon)

Reign and Elevation

Each astrological planet has one or two astrological sign(s) in which it is at home and where it "reigns." But almost all the planets have an additional sign in which they are elevated. Even though it is not well known, this "elevation" of the planets has been part of the classical tools in astrology for a long time. Taking "elevation" into consideration will give you more of an understanding of the characteristics of the astrological signs as well as of the planets.

The respective planet and the astrological sign are especially strong in the elevated position. The following list is a compilation of the accepted elevations:

Planet	reigns	and is elevated in
Sun	Leo	Aries
Mercury	Gemini and Virgo	Virgo
Venus	Taurus and Libra	Pisces
Moon	Cancer	Taurus
Mars	Aries	Capricorn
Jupiter	Sagittarius	Cancer
Uranus	Aquarius	Scorpio
Neptune	Pisces	Cancer
Pluto	Scorpio	Leo

Ten-Day Cycle and Your Cards

Another classical instrument in astrology is the division of the year into thirty-six 10-day segments. Each astrological sign contains three 10-day segments and each segment has a "10-day ruler." The tradition we use in this book is known as "Hellenistic astrology," although there are other methods, such as "Indian astrology."

The following is a journey through a year's cycle:

Spring 10-Day Cycle

3.21–3.31
Mars in Aries
II-Wands

4.1–4.10
Sun in Aries
III-Wands

4.11–4.20
Venus in Aries
IV-Wands

4.21–4.30
Mercury in Taurus
V-Pentacles (V-Disks)

5.1–5.10
Moon in Taurus
VI-Pentacles (VI-Disks)

5.11–5.20
Saturn in Taurus
VII-Pentacles (VII-Disks)

5.21–5.31
Jupiter in Gemini
VIII-Swords

6.1–6.10
Mars in Gemini
IX-Swords

6.11–6.21
Sun in Gemini
X-Swords

Summer 10-Day Cycle

6.22–7.1
Venus in Cancer
II-Cups

7.2–7.12
Mercury in Cancer
III-Cups

7.13–7.22
Moon in Cancer
IV-Cups

7.23–8.2
Saturn in Leo
V-Wands

8.3–8.12
Jupiter in Leo
VI-Wands

8.13–8.22
Mars in Leo
VII-Wands

8.23–9.2
Sun in Gemini
VIII-Pentacles (VIII-Disks)

9.3–9.12
Venus in Gemini
IX-Pentacles (IX-Disks)

9.13–9.22
Mercury in Gemini
X-Pentacles (X-Disks)

Fall 10-Day Cycle

9.23–10.2
Moon in Libra
II-Swords

10.3–10.12
Saturn in Libra
III-Swords

10.13–10.22
Jupiter in Libra
IV-Swords

10.23–11.1
Mars in Scorpio
V-Cups

11.2–11.11
Sun in Scorpio
VI-Cups

11.12–11.21
Venus in Scorpio
VII-Cups

11.22–12.1
Mercury in Sagittarius
VIII-Wands

12.2–12.11
Moon in Sagittarius
IX-Wands

12.12–12.20
Saturn in Sagittarius
X-Wands

Winter 10-Day Cycle

12.21–12.30
Jupiter in Capricorn
II-Pentacles (II-Disks)

12.31–1.9
Mars in Capricorn
III-Pentacles (III-Disks)

1.10–1.19
Sun in Capricorn
IV-Pentacles (IV-Disks)

1.20–1.29
Venus in Aquarius
V-Swords

1.30–2.8
Mercury in Aquarius
VI-Swords

2.9–2.18
Moon in Aquarius
VII-Swords

2.19–2.28/2.29
Saturn in Pisces
VIII-Cups

3.1–3.10
Jupiter in Pisces
IX-Cups

3.11–3.20
Mars in Pisces
X-Cups

OVERVIEW

Date	Astrological Sign	Major Card	Court Card
3.21–4.20	Aries	IV-The Emperor	Queen of Wands
4.21–5.20	Taurus	V-The Hierophant	King of Pentacles (Prince of Disks)
5.21–6.21	Gemini	VI-The Lovers	Knight of Swords
6.22–7.22	Cancer	VII-The Chariot	Queen of Cups
7.23–8.22	Leo	VIII-Strength (XI-Lust)	King of Wands (Prince of Wands)
8.23–9.22	Virgo	IX-The Hermit	Knight of Pentacles (Knight of Disks)
9.23–10.22	Libra	XI-Justice (VIII-Adjustment)	Queen of Swords
10.23–11.21	Scorpio	XIII-Death	King of Cups (Prince of Cups)
11.22–12.20	Sagittarius	XIV-Temperance (Art)	Knight of Wands
12.21–1.19	Capricorn	XV-The Devil	Queen of Pentacles (Queen of Disks)
1.20–2.18	Aquarius	XVII-The Star	King of Swords (Prince of Swords)
2.19–3.20	Pisces	XVIII-The Moon	Knight of Cups

Numbered Cards	Reigning Planet Card	Card of the "Elevated" Planet
II–IV Wands	XVI-The Tower	XIX-The Sun
V–VII Pentacles/ V–VII Disks	III-The Empress	II-The High Priestess (The Priestess)
VIII–X Swords	I-Magician (The Magus)	—
II–IV Cups	II-The High Priestess	X-Wheel of Fortune (Fortune) and XII-The Hanged Man
V–VII Wands	XIX-The Sun	XX-Judgment (The Aeon)
VIII–X Pentacles/ VIII–X Disks	I-The Magician (The Magus)	I-The Magician (The Magus)
II–IV Swords	III-The Empress	XXI-The World (The Universe)
V–VII Cups	XX-Judgment (The Aeon)	XXII/0-The Fool
VIII–X Wands	X-Wheel of Fortune (Fortune)	—
II–IV Pentacles/ II–IV Disks	XXI-The World (The Universe)	XVI-The Tower
V–VII Swords	XXII/0-The Fool	—
VIII–X Cups	XII-The Hanged Man	III-The Empress

Astrological Definition of Tarot Cards

Major Arcana/Trump Cards

I-The Magician (The Magus) .... Mercury
II-The High Priestess (The Priestess) .... Moon
III-The Empress .... Venus
IV-The Emperor .... Aries
V-The Hierophant .... Taurus
VI-The Lovers .... Gemini
VII-The Chariot .... Cancer
VIII/XI-Strength (Lust) .... Leo
IX-The Hermit .... Virgo
X-Wheel of Fortune (Fortune) .... Jupiter
XI/VIII-Justice (Adjustment) .... Libra
XII-The Hanged Man .... Neptune
XIII-Death .... Scorpio
XIV-Temperance (Art) .... Sagittarius
XV-The Devil .... Capricorn
XVI-The Tower .... Mars
XVII-The Star .... Aquarius
XVIII-The Moon .... Pisces
XIX-The Sun .... Sun
XX-Judgment (The Aeon) .... Pluto
XXI-The World (The Universe) .... Saturn
0/XXII-The Fool .... Uranus

Wands

Queen of Wands . . . . Aries
King/Prince of Wands . . . . Leo
Knight of Wands . . . . Sagittarius
Page/Princess of Wands . . . . Beginning of Spring
Ace of Wands . . . . Fire
II of Wands . . . . Mars in Aries
III of Wands . . . . Sun in Aries
IV of Wands . . . . Venus in Aries
V of Wands . . . . Saturn in Leo
VI of Wands . . . . Jupiter in Leo
VII of Wands . . . . Mars in Leo
VIII of Wands . . . . Mercury in Sagittarius
IX of Wands . . . . Moon in Sagittarius
X of Wands . . . . Saturn in Sagittarius

Cups

Queen of Cups . . . . Cancer
King of Cups . . . . Scorpio
Knight of Cups . . . . Pisces
Page/Princess of Cups . . . . Beginning of Summer
Ace of Cups . . . . Water
II of Cups . . . . Venus in Cancer
III of Cups . . . . Mercury in Cancer
IV of Cups . . . . Moon in Cancer
V of Cups . . . . Mars in Scorpio
VI of Cups . . . . Sun in Scorpio
VII of Cups . . . . Venus in Scorpio
VIII of Cups . . . . Saturn in Pisces
IX of Cups . . . . Jupiter in Pisces
X of Cups . . . . Mars in Pisces

Swords

Queen of Swords .... Libra
King of Swords .... Aquarius
Knight of Swords .... Gemini
Page/Princess of Swords .... Beginning of Fall
Ace of Swords .... Air
II of Swords .... Moon in Libra
III of Swords .... Saturn in Libra
IV of Swords .... Jupiter in Libra
V of Swords .... Venus in Aquarius
VI of Swords .... Mercury in Aquarius
VII of Swords .... Moon in Aquarius
VIII of Swords .... Jupiter in Gemini
IX of Swords .... Mars in Gemini
X of Swords .... Sun in Gemini

Pentacles/Disks

Queen of Pentacles/Disks .... Sagittarius
King of Pentacles/Disks .... Taurus
Knight of Pentacles/Disks .... Gemini
Page/Princess of Pentacles/Disks ...... Beginning of Winter
Ace of Pentacles/Disks .... Earth
II of Pentacles/Disks .... Jupiter in Capricorn
III of Pentacles/Disks .... Mars in Capricorn
IV of Pentacles/Disks .... Sun in Capricorn
V of Pentacles/Disks .... Mercury in Taurus
VI of Pentacles/Disks .... Moon in Taurus
VII of Pentacles/Disks .... Saturn in Taurus
VIII of Pentacles/Disks .... Sun in Virgo
IX of Pentacles/Disks .... Venus in Virgo
X of Pentacles/Disks .... Mercury in Virgo

Further Applications

You now have one or more Tarot cards for every planet, 10-day cycle, and especially astrological sign to use as visual/symbolic guidelines. Accept any contradictions that you may find between the astrological and Tarot symbols. For instance, Saturn is often considered "a grouchy old man," which does not fit with the Tarot card "XXI-The World" (The Universe). However, the meaning of Saturn/Cronus in mythology and the "XXI-The World" card are much more diverse and have more in common than what you might find at first glance.

Be open yet careful when you combine astrological concepts and Tarot card images. Their association will gain in dimension. Search for them and let yourself be inspired.

"Borderline Cases": Between Two Astrological Signs

The transition date, or the date that makes the change from one astrological sign to the next, differs at times. If you were born on September 23, you will find that you are sometimes considered a "Virgo" and other times a "Libra."

One thing is certain: birthdays and other events that fall directly or shortly before or after such dates are always influenced by the transition from one sign to the next. For example, the transition from Aquarius to Pisces (approximately February 18 to February 19) means the transition from "knowledge" to "belief" (definition for Aquarius: "I know"; for Pisces: "I believe").

The transition from one astrological sign to the next is also determined by a specific theme. Therefore, whoever deals with such dates is also influenced by this theme.

The Range Within an Astrological Sign

Knowing the traditional 10-day cycle tells you the differences as well as the range within each astrological sign. This gives you the opportunity to further examine the meaning of the astrological messages.

The Quality of Time—the Magic of the Moment

Look at the whole profile of the traditional 10-day cycle step-by-step throught the year. Use the respective cards of the present cycle and watch what kind of themes and chances the current cycle offers you personally.

**Your Personal
Lucky Card**

Here is a way you can incorporate astrology into the determination of your personal Lucky Card:

Put out the Major Card that belongs to your astrological sign as well as the one that belongs to your ascendant. The sum of these two cards gives you a third Major Card, which is your personal lucky card.

Example: Aries + ascendant Taurus = personal lucky card "IX-The Hermit." Aries = Major Card IV; Taurus = Major Card V. IV + V = IX-The Hermit.

Taurus + ascendant Sagittarius = personal lucky card "XIX-The Sun." Taurus = Major Card V; Sagittarius = Major Card XIV; V + XIV = XIX-The Sun.

Scorpio + ascendant Cancer = personal lucky card "XX-Judgment." Scorpio = Major Card XIII; Cancer = Major Card VII. XIII + VII = XX-Judgment.

If the sum of the respective Major Cards is greater than twenty-two, do not use the sum-of-the-digit method. Instead, work within the cycle of the Major Arcana Cards and continue counting.

Example: Aquarius + ascendant Capricorn = personal lucky card "X-Wheel of Fortune." Aquarius = Major Card XVII; Capricorn = Major Card XV; XVII + XV = XXXII = XXII + X. Go through the whole circle of the Major Arcana Cards once and then add ten.

Pisces + ascendant Gemini = personal lucky card "II-The High Priestess." Pisces = Major Card XVIII; Gemini = Major Card VI; XVIII + VI = XXIV = XXII + II.

Virgo + ascendant Aquarius = personal lucky card "IV-The Emperor." Virgo = Major Card IX; Aquarius = Major Card XVII; IX + XVII = XXVI = XXII + IV.

See page 28 for more on Lucky Cards.

Index